'A treasure trove of poetic [...]

'*The Fire of Joy* is a proper [...] and persuasive. James love [...] and, by the end, the layman certainly loves James . . . "It's a dipper," said my husband, reading over my shoulder. If I wasn't on review duty, that's the way I'd read it: dipping in at random, at bedtime, a poem a night.'   Laura Freeman, *The Times*

'*The Fire of Joy* is a set of personal, quintessentially Jamesian commentaries on 80 of his favourite poems.'   *Guardian*

'A must for anthology lovers . . . The late, great critic and poet doesn't so much look forward as back; these are old favourites (Byron, Wordsworth, Masefield, Owen) from a lifetime's reading, with personal notes on each one. I found it moving as well as a joy.'   Bel Mooney, *Daily Mail*

'A wonderful anthology of 80 or so poems to memorise and read aloud, selected by the late critic and humorist Clive James. Enjoy the poems and his witty, opinionated mini-essays about his choices.'   *The Times*, 'Best Books of 2020 So Far . . .'

'Clive James's joyous farewell . . . from Thomas Wyatt to Carol Ann Duffy, this valedictory volume features 80 poems he learned and loved, each accompanied by an essay to persuade us of their brilliance.'

Rishi Dastidar, *Guardian, Best Poetry of 2020*

'Clive James was so prolific that he's still publishing books a year after his death . . . [These] are poems to "murmur under your breath at the bus stop, declaim aloud in the bath, roar from the rooftops".'   James Marriott, *The Times*,
'Best Literary Non-fiction Books of the Year 2020'

'A book to lighten the darkness . . . What links them all [the selected poems] are Clive James's typically witty, sometimes abrasive and always passionate comments. It's a book to dip into and ponder in this bleak midwinter.'   Piers Plowright, *Tablet*

'Extraordinarily cogent . . . I have read many old men's books over the years, and even the best writers often lose their flavour . . . But this book shows no diminution whatever of James's talents, and it's fuelled by his obvious love of the form.'

Marcus Berkmann, *Spectator*

'[This book] is full of boisterous life . . . His farewell is funny, intellectually sharp and a faithful companion for this age of turmoil and uncertainty . . . [it] rings and rhymes with passion and learning from a big brain who found room in his soul for poetry and in his heart for the contentment it can bring in good times and the solace it carries in bad times.'

Hugh MacDonald, *Herald*

'The context of [this book's] composition is inescapable and each choice seems more moving in light of James's impending demise . . . *The Fire of Joy* is a generous and genial valediction from one of Australia's most famous wits.'

James Antoniou, *Sydney Morning Herald*

'A deeply affecting book that blends autobiography with literary criticism, and is filled with James's trademark breezy erudition and wit . . . It is indeed a joy to read, and savour.'

Troy Bramston, *Weekend Australian*

The Fire of Joy

Clive James was the multi-million-copy bestselling author of more than forty books. His poetry collection *Sentenced to Life* and his translation of Dante's *The Divine Comedy* were both *Sunday Times* top ten bestsellers, and his collections of verse were shortlisted for many prizes. In 2012 he was appointed CBE and in 2013 an Officer of the Order of Australia. He died in 2019.

ALSO BY CLIVE JAMES

AUTOBIOGRAPHY

The Complete Unreliable Memoirs Volume One: Unreliable Memoirs, Falling Towards England, and *May Week Was In June* · *The Complete Unreliable Memoirs Volume Two: North Face of Soho* and *The Blaze of Obscurity*

FICTION

Brilliant Creatures · *The Remake*
Brrm! Brrm! · *The Silver Castle*

VERSE

Other Passports: Poems 1958–1985
The Book of My Enemy: Collected Verse 1958–2003
Opal Sunset: Selected Poems 1958–2008
Angels Over Elsinore: Collected Verse 2003–2008
Nefertiti in the Flak Tower: Collected Verse 2008–2011
Sentenced to Life · *Collected Poems 1958–2015*
Gate of Lilacs · *Injury Time* · *The River in the Sky*

TRANSLATION

The Divine Comedy

CRITICISM

The Metropolitan Critic (new edition, 1994)
Visions Before Midnight · *The Crystal Bucket*
First Reactions (US) · *From the Land of Shadows*
Glued to the Box · *Snakecharmers in Texas*
The Dreaming Swimmer · *Fame in the 20th Century*
On Television · *Even As We Speak* · *Reliable Essays*
As of This Writing (US) · *The Meaning of Recognition*
Cultural Amnesia · *The Revolt of the Pendulum*
A Point of View · *Cultural Cohesion* · *Poetry Notebook*
Latest Readings · *Play All*
Somewhere Becoming Rain

TRAVEL

Flying Visits

CLIVE JAMES

The Fire of Joy

Roughly 80 Poems to Get by Heart
and Say Aloud

PICADOR

First published 2020 by Picador

First published in paperback 2020 by Picador

This edition first published 2022 by Picador
an imprint of Pan Macmillan
The Smithson, 6 Briset Street, London EC1M 5NR
EU representative: Macmillan Publishers Ireland Ltd, 1st Floor,
The Liffey Trust Centre, 117–126 Sheriff Street Upper,
Dublin 1, D01 YC43
Associated companies throughout the world
www.panmacmillan.com

ISBN 978-1-5290-4210-8

Copyright © Clive James 2020
Afterword copyright © Claerwen James 2020

The right of Clive James to be identified as the
author of this work has been asserted by him in accordance
with the Copyright, Designs and Patents Act 1988.

The permissions on pages 319–21 are an extension of this copyright page.

All rights reserved. No part of this publication may be reproduced,
stored in a retrieval system, or transmitted, in any form, or by any means
(electronic, mechanical, photocopying, recording or otherwise)
without the prior written permission of the publisher.

Pan Macmillan does not have any control over, or any responsibility for,
any author or third-party websites referred to in or on this book.

1 3 5 7 9 8 6 4 2

A CIP catalogue record for this book is available from the British Library.

Typeset in Minion Pro by Palimpsest Book Production Ltd, Falkirk, Stirlingshire
Printed and bound by CPI Group (UK) Ltd, Croydon, CR0 4YY

This book is sold subject to the condition that it shall not, by way of
trade or otherwise, be lent, hired out, or otherwise circulated without
the publisher's prior consent in any form of binding or cover other than
that in which it is published and without a similar condition including
this condition being imposed on the subsequent purchaser.

Visit **www.picador.com** to read more about all our books
and to buy them. You will also find features, author interviews and
news of any author events, and you can sign up for e-newsletters
so that you're always first to hear about our new releases.

To the next generation

"*The race of men*
Is like the generations of the leaves —
They fall in autumn to return in spring"
— Homer

Contents

Introduction

The French expression *feu de joie* refers to a military celebration when all the riflemen of a regiment fire one shot after another, in close succession: ideally the sound should be continuous, like a drum-roll. I first saw a *feu de joie* performed at an Australian Army Tattoo, in the main arena at the Sydney Showground, while I was still in short trousers. Later on, when I was doing National Service in longer trousers, I saw the ceremony performed again, on the parade ground in Ingleburn, New South Wales, in 1958. Symbolically, the fire of joy is a reminder that the regiment's collective power relies on the individual, and vice versa.

Imprinted on my mind, the succession of explosions became for me an evocation of the heritage of English poets and poetry, from Chaucer onwards. It still strikes me as a handy metaphor for the poetic succession, especially because, in the *feu de joie*, nobody got hurt. It was all noise: and noise, I believe, is the first and last thing that poetry is. If a poem doesn't sound compelling, it won't continue to exist. This is an especially important thing to say in the present era, when the pseudo-modernist idea still persists that there might be something sufficiently fascinating about the way that words are arranged on the page.

The main purpose of this book, then, is to provide ammunition that will satisfy the reader's urge to get on his or her feet and declaim. Even the most shy young people, in my experience, have this desire, although they might suppress it for fear of

1

making clowns of themselves. With a poem the most important thing is the way it sounds when you say it. At that rate even the most elementary nursery rhyme has it all over the kind of over-stuffed epic that needs ten pages of notes for every page of text, and reduces all who read it to paralysed slumber – or even worse, to a bogus admiration.

My understanding of what a poem is has been formed over a lifetime by the memory of the poems I love; the poems, or fragments of poems, that got into my head seemingly of their own volition, despite all the contriving powers of my natural idleness to keep them out. I discovered early on that a scrap of language can be like a tune in that respect: it gets into your head no matter what. In fact, I believe that is the true mark of poetry: you remember it despite yourself.

The Italians have a word for the store of poems you have in your head: a *gazofilacio*. To the English ear it might sound like an inadvisable amatory practice involving gasoline, but in its original language it actually means a treasure chamber of the mind. The poems I remember are the milestones marking the journey of my life. And unlike paintings, sculptures or passages of great music, they do not outstrip the scope of memory, but are the actual thing, incarnate.

With the contagious crackle of the *feu de joie* still rattling in my ears, let me flash back to Opportunity School at Hurstville, Sydney, whose supposedly playful regime was symbolised by its rule that every pupil, at the end of the day, had to stand beside his desk and recite a memorised poem before he was allowed to go home. It was a fantastic combination of Parnassus and a maximum-security prison. I usually managed to get an Early Mark, not just because my memory was good, but because I was lucky in the draw, being assigned poems that were hard to forget.

The remarkable thing, I suppose, is not that I memorised a few poems, but that I never forgot them. Perhaps because the reward for success was freedom, I thought of poetry, forever afterwards, as my ticket out: the equivalent of hiding in the laundry in the truck out of the prison camp. When I am busy with the eternal task of memorising chunks of Milton, I can hear the sirens as I escape through the woods outside the wire of Stalag Luft III. For me poetry means freedom. Even today, in fact especially today, when the ruins of my very body are the prison, poetry is my way through the wire and out into the world.

Later on, during my first year as an Arts student at Sydney University, the excellent lecturers in English heavily emphasised the truism that English poetry had not started from nowhere and from nothing, but had started in England at the time of Chaucer. This was an especially important idea to absorb when you could practically hear the Pacific surf crashing on the beach only a mile or two from the lecture room. The key notion was one of development: poetry from Chaucer onwards had been written by people who had read the poets who came before them. It was a story of someone writing something wonderful, and someone else coming along, reading it, and feeling impelled to write something even more wonderful. Even behind Chaucer there might have been another poet (I privately called him Robin Rimefellow) who invented the couplet, or anyway at least half of it.

I met actual living poets during the first week at university. They were fellow students. By the second week, I too was wearing a long scarf, baggy khaki drills, the soft desert boots that were called brothel-creepers, and carrying an armful of books by Ezra Pound. I decided to become a poet, although there was nothing bold about this decision, as it was already clear, even to me, that I was useless for anything else. The poet, in my view, is the kind of time-waster who thinks he is doing something crucial with the time he wastes: steering it towards eternity perhaps, or getting an Early Mark.

Smart teachers view the young poets with despair, but even smarter teachers realise there is something essential about them. If a university does not produce the occasional eloquent skiver, or unquenchably verbal time-waster, it is not fulfilling its true end. Almost all universities will somehow enforce the requirement for the student to study poetry, but they couldn't enforce the creation of it even if they had tyrannical powers. Although we, the poets, pursued the common fantasy that we were somehow cooperating in an eternal creative venture, we were competing like hell: a microcosm of the perpetual poetic desire to cap the other guy's effort with something even better.

That line of fire that continues past you, leading into the distance, is as bound to continue as you are not. Creativity is the great mystery. Anyone can be destructive, but the capacity to build something will go on being the great human surprise. The flashing fires of the poems we can't help remembering are clear proof of that.

Rules on Reading Aloud

1. Go more slowly than you think you need to. It's because you're ahead of yourself that you stumble.

2. In any regular stanza, pause for the length of a comma at the end of the line to indicate that the line is turning over. If there is already a comma there, pause for the length of two commas. Pause also for two comma lengths at the end of any line ending with a semi-colon, colon or full stop. Pause for at least three comma lengths between stanzas. Don't be afraid about the pauses losing you the audience. The impetus of the line will keep them listening, whereas a stumble from too much gabble will very soon make them wonder why they didn't stay at home and watch television.

3. Keep your voice up towards the end of the line. There is no point starting a line strongly if you swallow the end of it, and you are more likely to swallow it if you assume that the audience already knows what you are about to say. The audience is not psychic.

4. No amount of vocal beauty will compensate for the unfortunate fact that you have no idea what the poem means. Figure it out before you start.

5. If you are reading in public, with a microphone, make sure you attend the microphone test, even if it takes place hours before. Nothing ruins a reading more thoroughly than a lot of bang-thump-bang-thump-sorry. Once you

are in front of the microphone and speaking, it isn't necessary to ask the audience if they can hear you. If they can't, they will tell you.

6. Linking patter breaks the mood. Keep it to a minimum, keep it factual and follow the rule of never underestimating the intelligence of the audience, while never overestimating what they know. Don't upstage your own poetry by making the prose commentary more relaxed and inventive than the poem.

Western Wind

ANONYMOUS

Western wind when wilt thou blow
that the small rain down can rain.
Christy, if my love were in my arms
and I in my bed again.

———◆———

NOBODY KNOWS WHO WROTE IT, BUT THAT IN ITSELF
could be stated as an ideal of English poetry: the best poems
seem all to have been written by the one sensitive, sensible per-
sonality. Even the extravagant poets like Milton, Swinburne and
Hopkins don't stray all that far from ordinary language, and
what makes them poetic is their vision more than their quirky
diction.

Back beyond Chaucer, who can be said to have started the
fashion for poets having names, this poem must have got into
the heads of everyone who heard it. Probably it still does.

My guess is that it was written by a woman. One assumes,
here, that the narrator and the poet are one and the same, but
the assumption seems fair, unless there were already poets on
council grants wandering around and observing women in a
local setting. And if it was composed by a woman, she wasn't the
lady of a grand house; she's out there in the weather. What can
get her warm again? Enter the lover. This neat little poem is

packed with drama, like a tiny purse full of gold. One way or another, most good poems do have drama. And usually the story is the first thing to look for. There are famous poems that have no story but they are getting closer to being just words, which is always a dangerous lure for a poet. If poetry were just words almost anyone could do it.

This poem loses nothing by being anonymous. Sometimes I think of it as having been written by myself, halfway up an orchard ladder, and shivering in a pair of self-darned tights.

They Flee From Me

SIR THOMAS WYATT
1535

They flee from me that sometime did me seek
With naked foot, stalking in my chamber.
I have seen them gentle, tame, and meek,
That now are wild and do not remember
That sometime they put themself in danger
To take bread at my hand; and now they range,
Busily seeking with a continual change.

Thanked be fortune it hath been otherwise
Twenty times better; but once in special,
In thin array after a pleasant guise,
When her loose gown from her shoulders did fall,
And she me caught in her arms long and small;
Therewithal sweetly did me kiss
And softly said, 'Dear heart, how like you this?'

It was no dream: I lay broad waking.
But all is turned thorough my gentleness
Into a strange fashion of forsaking;
And I have leave to go of her goodness,
And she also, to use newfangleness.
But since that I so kindly am served
I would fain know what she hath deserved.

———

From the sheer delicious sound of its opening lines, the poem equals the visual charm of a courtly young man painted in miniature by Hilliard, but the poem soon turns out to be quite hard to say. Wyatt was an important pioneer of the Petrarchan sonnet in English. This, however, is not a sonnet (it's an extravaganza in the style known as 'rhyme royal') though it might pass for a sonnet if the last stanza were removed. Such a truncation, however, would remove a highly interesting development, and anyway it would not do anything to give the second last line of the second stanza the fifth beat it is missing, and which it needs in order to be smoothly said.

From the formal viewpoint, then, the poem is best regarded initially as a collection of pretty lines, and some of them pretty marvellous: so marvellous, in fact, that it speaks to anyone, no matter what gender they are, who has been taught bitter lessons by love. In the poem, however, it's definitely a bloke, and he's on the ropes.

The women in the poem are upmarket. The 'thin array' was a social signifier at a time of coarse cloth and sumptuary laws, and the arms long and small indicate a delicacy and refinement of a social world from which our swain would not wish to be cast down. One of the women, in particular – the 'once in special' angel of the second stanza – can be quickly apprehended as a woman powerful enough to make her favour a blessing if she hands it out, and a disaster if she withdraws it. The third stanza proves that she has withdrawn it, and left him sick enough to toy with fancies of revenge.

But he is only thinking that: because if the mere existence of the poem proves that he is troubled, the language in which it is written proves him gentle. Too gentle, perhaps: in the third stanza we discover that his finer feelings might have worked against his interests, and doomed him to 'a strange fashion of forsaking': every man's suspicion, from that day to this, that the love-spell can be dispelled by too much pondering on the event. Men who have lost the game through their stupidity often prefer to believe that they lost it through their decency. Shakespeare condensed all shades of that disappointment into Henry V's great observation, in Act V Scene 2 of his play, that these fellows who rhyme their way into a lady's favour do often reason themselves out again.

This is a lot to pick up on a first reading, especially when the wording is seductive enough to ensure that every reading is a first reading. When I first read the poem, in Sydney in the late 1950s, I was stopped almost straight away by the combination in the second line of 'with naked foot' and 'stalking in my chamber'. Wyatt couldn't have been thinking, as I immediately did, about a stalking leopard from *Mogambo* or *Where No Vultures Fly*, but he was certainly thinking about lending power to the naked foot: so the polarity of the narrator's attitude towards the objects of his desire is already there in the first instance. He might want them, but a lot might depend on whether they want him.

I myself, at that stage of my life, was still in the painful process of finding out that women do the deciding, so that this poem was part of my education; and I could tell it was, even at the time. That tone of voice, the tone of tutelary experience, runs right through English literature. Philip Larkin in his late middle age was still haunted by 'the wonderful feel of girls'. He didn't say the wonderful feel of women. But he didn't mind about being politically incorrect, and anyway he was harking back to childhood – which is the framework into which love puts you, aching for comfort.

Elegy

CHIDIOCK TICHBORNE
1586

My prime of youth is but a frost of cares,
My feast of joy is but a dish of paine,
My crop of corne is but a field of tares,
And al my good is but vaine hope of gaine.
The day is past, and yet I saw no sunne,
And now I live, and now my life is done.

My tale was heard, and yet it was not told,
My fruite is falne, & yet my leaves are greene:
My youth is spent, and yet I am not old,
I saw the world, and yet I was not seene.
My thred is cut, and yet it is not spunne,
And now I live, and now my life is done.

I sought my death, and found it in my wombe,
I lookt for life, and saw it was a shade:
I trod the earth, and knew it was my tombe,
And now I die, and now I was but made.
My glasse is full, and now my glasse is runne,
And now I live, and now my life is done.

THE FIRST WORD FOR THIS POEM IS 'FANTASTIC'. CHIDIOCK Tichborne was either only twenty-eight when he was executed for his part in the Babington Plot to assassinate Elizabeth I, or else even younger. He wrote this poem just before he died. Dr Johnson said that when a man knows he is about to die, it concentrates the mind wonderfully. I am bound to say that I have found the opposite. The prospect of my own oblivion helped give me some perspective on just what Chidiock Tichborne achieved during his brief but final time in the Tower.

He did it with extreme simplicity of language, as if determined to avoid the metaphysical complexity that was already fashionable. John Donne, for example, might have taken a longer and more twisty path towards clarity. But there is a lot of argument packed into the line about the leaves still being green although the fruit is fallen; it's a perfect way of saying that your life is over before it has begun. 'My thred is cut, and yet it is not spunne' might or might not be an allusion to the three Fates of Greek myth, but it is certainly a chilling way of saying that the speaker is finished before he starts. The true miracle of the poem is that he could see all that and say all that with the axe hanging over his head. Or in fact, something much worse than an axe. They were terrible times, but somehow they produced a purity of language like this.

The Lie

SIR WALTER RALEIGH
1592–4

Go, soul, the body's guest,
Upon a thankless errand;
Fear not to touch the best;
The truth shall be thy warrant.
Go, since I needs must die,
And give the world the lie.

Say to the court, it glows
And shines like rotten wood;
Say to the church, it shows
What's good, and doth no good.
If church and court reply,
Then give them both the lie.

Tell potentates, they live
Acting by others' action;
Not loved unless they give,
Not strong but by a faction.
If potentates reply,
Give potentates the lie.

Tell men of high condition,
That manage the estate,
Their purpose is ambition,
Their practice only hate.

And if they once reply,
Then give them all the lie.

Tell them that brave it most,
They beg for more by spending,
Who, in their greatest cost,
Seek nothing but commending.
And if they make reply,
Then give them all the lie.

Tell zeal it wants devotion;
Tell love it is but lust;
Tell time it is but motion;
Tell flesh it is but dust.
And wish them not reply,
For thou must give the lie.

Tell age it daily wasteth;
Tell honour how it alters;
Tell beauty how she blasteth;
Tell favour how it falters.
And as they shall reply,
Give every one the lie.

Tell wit how much it wrangles
In tickle points of niceness;
Tell wisdom she entangles
Herself in overwiseness.
And when they do reply,
Straight give them both the lie.

Tell physic of her boldness;
Tell skill it is pretension;
Tell charity of coldness;
Tell law it is contention.
And as they do reply,
So give them still the lie.

Tell fortune of her blindness;
Tell nature of decay;
Tell friendship of unkindness;
Tell justice of delay.
And if they will reply,
Then give them all the lie.

Tell arts they have no soundness,
But vary by esteeming;
Tell schools they want profoundness,
And stand too much on seeming.
If arts and schools reply,
Give arts and schools the lie.

Tell faith it's fled the city;
Tell how the country erreth;
Tell manhood shakes off pity;
Tell virtue least preferreth.
And if they do reply,
Spare not to give the lie.

So when thou hast, as I
Commanded thee, done blabbing –
Although to give the lie

Deserves no less than stabbing –
Stab at thee he that will,
No stab the soul can kill.

———

THE NOTION PERSISTS THAT ELIZABETH I WAS IN LOVE
with Sir Walter Raleigh. If she was, it was a tough love: she
dumped him in the Tower and he was still there when her suc-
cessor finally got around to killing him.

As he rotted in his cell, Raleigh would have been well justified
in pointing out that he actually did do all those things: went to
America, fought the Spanish Armada, brought back to the
Queen some of her most precious treasures. Really, when you
think of the track record of that useless bastard Essex . . .

Raleigh should have been royalty. His last letter to his wife,
written in the Tower of London just before his execution, is
proof of that. 'Time and death call me away': he could speak like
a king. Instead, he was killed by one: though Raleigh had some-
how survived being loved by Elizabeth, he could not survive the
determination of James to execute him as a sop to the Spaniards.
But even when he had seen the axe – 'this is a sharp medicine'
– he was not unmanned by fear.

Indeed fear, if he felt it, seemed to make him even more of a
man than he was. Like Chidiock Tichborne, well known for only
one poem, Raleigh, well known for several poems even at the
time, had the knack of keeping his mind in one piece even at
the moment when it was about to be separated from the rest of
his body.

In Raleigh's youth, Ben Jonson was his tutor, but there are

qualities of perception that no amount of tutoring can instil. That metaphor about the glow of rotting wood probably depends on a direct perception, although whether the perception happened in South America or in his backyard at home there is no telling.

Raleigh remains, to this day, one of the most daunting examples of the poet for whom poetry isn't everything. We should note carefully, however, that he was technically meticulous when he wrote it. On the whole it's probably more important to defeat the Spanish Armada, but that conclusion should perhaps not be reached too easily: it might be better to get your iambic trimeters in shape before the call to arms rings out in response to all those fires along the coast.

The expense of spirit in a waste of shame

(Sonnet 129)

WILLIAM SHAKESPEARE

1609

The expense of spirit in a waste of shame
Is lust in action; and till action, lust
Is perjured, murderous, bloody, full of blame,
Savage, extreme, rude, cruel, not to trust;
Enjoyed no sooner but despisèd straight:
Past reason hunted; and no sooner had,
Past reason hated, as a swallowed bait,
On purpose laid to make the taker mad:
Mad in pursuit, and in possession so;
Had, having, and in quest to have, extreme;
A bliss in proof, and proved, a very woe;
Before, a joy proposed; behind, a dream.
    All this the world well knows; yet none knows well
    To shun the heaven that leads men to this hell.

———

AND DOWN THE ROAD FROM STRATFORD CAME STRIDING
the man in tights. His career went on to prove that William
Shakespeare had more on his mind than just sex, but he was
sharp enough to notice from the beginning that for most people
it was the consuming preoccupation. Even amongst the vast
mass and variety of his work, the sheaf of sonnets stands out

because passion is the subject – the passion between people, and not just the mere passion to conquer Scotland, rule Denmark, etc.

We can be sure about his detachment from the topic even though we can't be quite sure about his sexual orientation. W.H. Auden, in his long introduction to his excellent edition of the *Sonnets*, boldly assumed that Shakespeare was gay, but Auden would have assumed that about 'Slapsie' Maxie Rosenbloom, who was still wrestling at Leichhardt Stadium in Sydney when I was a kid.

Remarkable for its technical assurance, this great sonnet is also remarkable for what it hasn't got. It's quite short of imagery: the madness-inducing bait, for example, is the most spectacular thing about it, and the bait just lies there. What drives the sonnet more than its pictures is its syntax. 'Past reason hunted' shades to 'past reason hated' like a champion skater turning on the spot. And at the end, 'All this the world well knows; yet none knows well' is a piece of symmetrical balancing that fairly aches to be released into the long relaxation of the last line.

After the virtuoso ending knocks us flat, it's time to get back to the start and realise that there was nothing simple about that either. And now we ask the question, 'What does it mean, exactly?' Scholars have gone on arguing the point, but our first answer is hard to quell: something is being irretrievably expended here. There is no mention of babies, or even, particularly, of pleasure. There is just the evocation of a process, but somehow we are led to believe that it is the process of life. Shakespeare might dream of its being more than that but he knows that the dream is part of the process too.

The last couplet is built much more out of syntax than out of metaphor. There is a tendency on the part of some critics and scholars to find that Shakespeare's clinching couplets are mere flourishes. So they often are, but no more so than a flourish with the hat as the actor steps elegantly backward from centre stage.

Note to reciters: there is an absolute necessity to pronounce the final 'e' in despisèd, otherwise the pentameter goes wrong.

Chorus Sacerdotum

FULKE GREVILLE
1609

O wearisome condition of humanity!
Born under one law, to another bound;
Vainly begot and yet forbidden vanity;
Created sick, commanded to be sound.
What meaneth nature by these diverse laws?
Passion and reason, self-division cause.
Is it the mark or majesty of power
To make offenses that it may forgive?
Nature herself doth her own self deflower
To hate those errors she herself doth give.
For how should man think that he may not do,
If nature did not fail and punish, too?
Tyrant to others, to herself unjust,
Only commands things difficult and hard,
Forbids us all things which it knows is lust,
Makes easy pains, unpossible reward.
If nature did not take delight in blood,
She would have made more easy ways to good.
We that are bound by vows and by promotion,
With pomp of holy sacrifice and rites,
To teach belief in good and still devotion,
To preach of heaven's wonders and delights;
Yet when each of us in his own heart looks
He finds the God there, far unlike his books.

WHEN I ARRIVED IN CAMBRIDGE AS AN UNDERGRADUATE, I was daunted to find myself compulsorily involved in a weekly practical-criticism class. At its first meeting the unseen text was this poem. By a remarkable stroke of luck, it was the only poem from the seventeenth century that I knew anything about, and I was even able to say the name of its author, Fulke Greville. Other students in the class, especially the Americans, were stunned. The lecturer taking the class went away with the illusion that I knew everything about the seventeenth century. In fact I barely knew that it followed the sixteenth century, but further study revealed that I had chosen my poem well.

The poem (which started life as a Chorus of Priests in Greville's play *Mustapha*) is all argument. There's scarcely an image in it. Usually felt as a deficiency, the absence of fantasy works in this poem as a pledge of dialectical seriousness. Every line is a quarrel, and every quarrel is a passage of action, so the whole thing is alive with conflict. Nowadays the conflict would be called the Human Condition – he seems to be in the process of inventing that deadly phrase in his very first line – but in those days there was still enough faith in belief, or belief in faith, to make it look like an urgent paradox that God's commands were so hard to obey. The idea that men might make verbal music out of the difficulties He had created was, however, still quite new in the world. Thought in the form of music: the very idea of such a thing was a consolation, even when it revealed itself as a source of anguish.

The Sun Rising

JOHN DONNE
1633

Busy old fool, unruly sun,
    Why dost thou thus,
Through windows, and through curtains call on us?
Must to thy motions lovers' seasons run?
    Saucy pedantic wretch, go chide
    Late schoolboys, and sour prentices,
  Go tell court huntsmen that the king will ride,
  Call country ants to harvest offices;
Love, all alike, no season knows nor clime,
Nor hours, days, months, which are the rags of time.

    Thy beams, so reverend and strong
    Why shouldst thou think?
I could eclipse and cloud them with a wink,
But that I would not lose her sight so long;
    If her eyes have not blinded thine,
    Look, and tomorrow late, tell me,
  Whether both th'Indias of spice and mine
  Be where thou leftst them, or lie here with me.
Ask for those kings whom thou saw'st yesterday,
And thou shalt hear, All here in one bed lay.

    She's all states, and all princes, I,
    Nothing else is.
Princes do but play us; compared to this,

All honour's mimic, all wealth alchemy.
 Thou, sun, art half as happy as we,
 In that the world's contracted thus.
Thine age asks ease, and since thy duties be
 To warm the world, that's done in warming us.
Shine here to us, and thou art everywhere;
This bed thy centre is, these walls, thy sphere.

———◆———

SOME OF THE KNOTTY PUZZLES THAT WERE PRESENTED BY the upsurge of metaphysical poetry are still being argued about centuries later, but Donne, than whom no one was knottier, wrote at least one poem, this one, which was plain sailing all the way. These walls are the world. A basic feeling of love, isn't it? 'She's all states, and all Princes, I / Nothing else is.' That notion gives her equal power: a charmingly humble moment from a poet more accustomed to giving orders.

There was some controversy about whether Donne was a Papist, but there is none at all about his stature as a poet: he was the top dog. The greatness of his stature is only emphasised by the fact that sometimes his imagery got out of hand. Reading another poem by him, 'The Ecstasy' ('Our eye-beams twisted, and did thread / Our eyes upon one double string;'), lovers might balk. The more accurately visualised the more repellent it is. The eyeballs on strings idea was explained to us at length when we were students, but I didn't like it then and I don't like it now – as I would have told him at the time had I been there at his elbow. 'Don't forget that people see what you say. Do you really want those eyeballs bouncing around for all eternity?' But he brushes me aside.

Love III

GEORGE HERBERT
1633

Love bade me welcome: yet my soul drew back,
  Guilty of dust and sin.
But quick-eyed Love, observing me grow slack
  From my first entrance in,
Drew nearer to me, sweetly questioning
  If I lacked anything.

'A guest,' I answered, 'worthy to be here':
  Love said, 'You shall be he.'
'I, the unkind, ungrateful? Ah, my dear,
  I cannot look on thee.'
Love took my hand, and smiling did reply,
  'Who made the eyes but I?'

'Truth, Lord; but I have marred them; let my shame
  Go where it doth deserve.'
'And know you not,' says Love, 'who bore the blame?'
  'My dear, then I will serve.'
'You must sit down,' says Love, 'and taste my meat.'
  So I did sit and eat.

In the long eye of history, it might seem that the self-contained English poem had to recover its confidence after the cataclysmic outburst of Shakespearian drama, but in fact the tradition of the short lyric, as George Herbert's teeming prolificacy proves, went on developing during Shakespeare's theatrical reign. Shakespeare himself, as well as perfecting the form of the five-act play, gave a tremendous boost to the short lyric poem, by writing a whole batch of sonnets full of unbeatable intricacies of form and argument. But we weren't there at the time, and if we had been, George Herbert might have appeared to us as a prodigy who was mapping out a new range for the short poem all by himself. Shakespeare had dialogues between kings, queens and usurpers. George Herbert had dialogues between himself and God.

In this encounter across a dining table, God is present, disguised as a concept: Love. Only later on in the poem does He appear as himself, at His full height of eloquence, and even then He is robed not so much in a panoply of glory as in an air of humility. It is hard not to think of Herbert's attitude as that of a child being taught something necessary to do, but difficult to grasp, such as the necessity to put one's toys away, and not leave the little red fire engine on the stairs so that the cleaner can step on it and plunge screaming to her death. God is the patient instructor.

Eventually God has implanted his whole message, and the narrator signs off on a brief encounter. Almost nothing has happened, except that everything has. God's grace has been registered as a generosity. If this had been a restaurant, God would have paid the bill, but probably the encounter is happening at God's house; somewhere not very pretentious perhaps, and certainly not lavish enough to merit description. The meal is just two people facing each other, except that one of them is a divinity. Herbert, the narrator, is mortal, except that he is more than mortal, after being so lavishly instructed. He has feasted on the instruction. It never hurts to be reminded that history consists largely of things that used to be different. Here we are given the transcript of an intricate, highly sophisticated mealtime conversation that all took place before the adoption of the fork.

Herbert was a prodigious inventor of poetic forms, but they were all self-contained. Except perhaps for 'The Church Porch', he wasn't interested in any epic that he couldn't get into a nutshell. The necessity to write a long poem either never occurred to him, or he deduced from his own proclivities that a long poem was exactly what his short poems were going to add up to. That indeed is the effect he gives.

Herbert's poems amount to a collection of sub-atomic particles, simultaneously tiny but massive; with the epic sweep of a star system seen from a distance, but with the intricate compression and gravity of an atomic nucleus. (His own collective title for the products of his unique specificity of poetic scope was 'The Temple'. But he could equally have called it 'The Cyclotron', 'The Collider' or 'The Particle-Accelerator'. He was just a few hundred years too early for the descriptors that would have fitted.)

It would be easy to recommend fistfuls of other poems by Herbert. Perhaps the one that a reader should look at next is 'The Flower'. Its form is tricky to the glance because of the way the short lines, and fragmentary lines, link up; but in fact the conversational flow is so simple to say that it falls naturally into one's memory. And some of the ideas are so enchanting that you find yourself wondering why someone so talented did not write, say, five-act plays about mad kings. But perhaps he is doing something equally meritorious, and even equally comprehensive. 'These are thy wonders, Lord of Love'. If he has not helped us see God, he has certainly helped us see flowers. Clear sight is no longer my great thing, but as I look out into the blur of my back garden, I can see them glowing.

Delight in Disorder

ROBERT HERRICK
1648

A sweet disorder in the dress
Kindles in clothes a wantonness;
A lawn about the shoulders thrown
Into a fine distraction;
An erring lace, which here and there
Enthrals the crimson stomacher;
A cuff neglectful, and thereby
Ribands to flow confusedly;
A winning wave, deserving note,
In the tempestuous petticoat;
A careless shoe-string, in whose tie
I see a wild civility:
Do more bewitch me, than when art
Is too precise in every part.

———

BACK IN THE DAY, WE HAD A FOOTLIGHTS NUMBER IN
which my friend Jonathan James-Moore, an extremely droll
fellow (gone now, alas), recited this poem from the front of the
stage with full orotund pomposity, while behind him a comely
pair of students, one male and one female, acted it out. They did
a fashion-parade mime routine while pointing out the various
sartorial features.

There was and is nothing funny about the poem itself – except perhaps the lawn thrown about the shoulders – but by the time Jonathan James-Moore and the two mannequins had finished with it, there were people in the audience rolling around with their knees up. None of them ever forgot the words but in later years I noticed that everyone was remembering the sweetness of the poem's argument rather than the absurdity of our staging. There was a lesson there; words live.

On His Blindness

JOHN MILTON

1652–5

When I consider how my light is spent
Ere half my days in this dark world and wide,
And that one talent which is death to hide
Lodg'd with me useless, though my soul more bent
To serve therewith my Maker, and present
My true account, lest he returning chide;
'Doth God exact day-labour, light denied?'
I fondly ask. But Patience to prevent
That murmur, soon replies: 'God doth not need
Either man's work or his own gifts; who best
Bear his mild yoke, they serve him best. His state
Is kingly. Thousands at his bidding speed
And post o'er land and ocean without rest:
They also serve who only stand and wait.'

———

I STARTED TO MEMORISE THIS LITTLE POEM OF MILTON'S
in order to postpone the moment when I would have to start
memorising *Paradise Lost*. There is always someone in the
English-speaking countries who can recite *Paradise Lost* from
memory but you wouldn't count on his having memorised much
of anything else. Milton himself had a mighty power of memory.
During the writing day he might dictate the latest few pages of

his epic to his writing staff, but he couldn't have done that if he had not first shaped the composition in his head; a feat all the more tremendous when you consider the formal complexity of any given passage. This sonnet is proof that his urge to complexity was grounded in the capacity to be relatively simple.

Though the opening argument is self-refuting – his one talent was so far from useless that he wrote whole pictures with it – it provides the perfect take-off point for a flight of fantasy in which God controls the actions of the human world, yet somehow the narrator, deprived of the means to act at all, contrives to serve Him instead of just standing around waiting.

And how does the narrator do that? By writing the poem, which theoretically he should not be able to do. The poem is thus a tightly packed paradox, and a powerful hint of what the poet might achieve if he took a few years and transmitted, *per media* his secretarial staff, an immortal epic, supplemented by a sheaf of long poems almost equally monumental, except a bit shorter. (My favourite of those is *Samson Agonistes*: 'Eyeless in Gaza at the mill with slaves' – what a line! And *Paradise Regained* has lines of such enchanting simplicity that they prove he was never complicated except at will. And . . . Come on, the man was a genius.) Like most people who are blessed, or cursed, with great powers of concentration he could be tough company, but pretending not to admire him is a waste of time.

The Definition of Love

ANDREW MARVELL
1681

My love is of a birth as rare
As 'tis for object strange and high;
It was begotten by Despair
Upon Impossibility.

Magnanimous Despair alone
Could show me so divine a thing
Where feeble Hope could ne'er have flown,
But vainly flapp'd its tinsel wing.

And yet I quickly might arrive
Where my extended soul is fixt,
But Fate does iron wedges drive,
And always crowds itself betwixt.

For Fate with jealous eye does see
Two perfect loves, nor lets them close;
Their union would her ruin be,
And her tyrannic pow'r depose.

And therefore her decrees of steel
Us as the distant poles have plac'd,
(Though love's whole world on us doth wheel)
Not by themselves to be embrac'd;

Unless the giddy heaven fall,
And earth some new convulsion tear;
And, us to join, the world should all
Be cramp'd into a planisphere.

As lines, so loves oblique may well
Themselves in every angle greet;
But ours so truly parallel,
Though infinite, can never meet.

Therefore the love which us doth bind,
But Fate so enviously debars,
Is the conjunction of the mind,
And opposition of the stars.

———

IF ANDREW MARVELL HAD BEEN CALLED ANDREW
Dullfellow his achievement might have seemed less wonderful
to posterity, but a poem like this suggests that he deserved his
name. A poet who can start a stanza with a word like 'magnani-
mous', and give all its syllables their correct weight, is sending a
signal that he can write anything. As properties for his brilliant
argument, his images were more brilliant still: the vainly flap-
ping tinsel wing of Hope is a poem all by itself.

The argument proceeds with dazzling clarity until it strikes
him as profitable to complicate it into a puzzle. If we have to stop
to think about the stanza that begins 'Unless the giddy heaven
fall,' it's because he wants us to. What is a planisphere? It's a star

chart. He's cramming a three-dimensional cosmic event into the thin thickness of a page.

Once he has given us the idea of the cosmos, the infinite parallel lines that never meet sound like a precise analogy, although in fact real astronomy, as opposed to astrology, was still quite new in his time. In its precise technical sense, the 'opposition of the stars' was a notion as fresh as sliced bread.

Tam o' Shanter

ROBERT BURNS
1790

When chapman billies leave the street,
And drouthy neebors, neebors meet,
As market-days are wearing late,
An' folk begin to tak the gate;
While we sit bousing at the nappy,
And getting fou and unco happy,
We think na on the lang Scots miles,
The mosses, waters, slaps and styles,
That lie between us and our hame,
Whare sits our sulky sullen dame,
Gathering her brows like gathering storm,
Nursing her wrath to keep it warm.

This truth fand honest Tam o' Shanter,
As he frae Ayr ae night did canter,
(Auld Ayr, wham ne'er a town surpasses,
For honest men and bonny lasses.)

O Tam! hadst thou but been sae wise,
As ta'en thy ain wife Kate's advice!
She tauld thee weel thou was a skellum,
A blethering, blustering, drunken blellum;
That frae November till October,
Ae market-day thou was nae sober;
That ilka melder, wi' the miller,

Thou sat as lang as thou had siller;
That every naig was ca'd a shoe on,
The smith and thee gat roaring fou on;
That at the L—d's house, even on Sunday,
Thou drank wi' Kirkton Jean till Monday.
She prophesied that late or soon,
Thou would be found deep drown'd in Doon;
Or catch'd wi' warlocks in the mirk,
By Alloway's auld haunted kirk.

Ah, gentle dames! it gars me greet,
To think how mony counsels sweet,
How mony lengthen'd sage advices,
The husband frae the wife despises!

But to our tale: Ae market-night,
Tam had got planted unco right;
Fast by an ingle, bleezing finely,
Wi' reaming swats, that drank divinely;
And at his elbow, Souter Johnny,
His ancient, trusty, drouthy crony;
Tam lo'ed him like a vera brither;
They had been fou for weeks thegither.
The night drave on wi' sangs and clatter;
And ay the ale was growing better:
The landlady and Tam grew gracious,
Wi' favours, secret, sweet, and precious:
The Souter tauld his queerest stories;
The landlord's laugh was ready chorus:
The storm without might rair and rustle,
Tam did na mind the storm a whistle.

Care, mad to see a man sae happy,
E'en drown'd himsel amang the nappy:
As bees flee hame wi' lades o' treasure,
The minutes wing'd their way wi' pleasure;
Kings may be blest, but Tam was glorious,
O'er a' the ills o' life victorious!

But pleasures are like poppies spread,
You seize the flower, its bloom is shed;
Or like the snow falls in the river,
A moment white – then melts for ever;
Or like the borealis race,
That flit ere you can point their place;
Or like the rainbow's lovely form
Evanishing amid the storm. –
Nae man can tether time or tide;
The hour approaches Tam maun ride;
That hour, o' night's black arch the key-stane,
That dreary hour he mounts his beast in;
And sic a night he taks the road in,
As ne'er poor sinner was abroad in.

The wind blew as 'twad blawn its last;
The rattling showers rose on the blast;
The speedy gleams the darkness swallow'd;
Loud, deep, and lang, the thunder bellow'd:
That night, a child might understand,
The Deil had business on his hand.

Weel mounted on his gray mare, Meg,
A better never lifted leg,

Tam skelpit on thro' dub and mire,
Despising wind, and rain, and fire;
Whiles holding fast his gude blue bonnet;
Whiles crooning o'er some auld Scots sonnet;
Whiles glowring round wi' prudent cares,
Lest bogles catch him unawares:
Kirk-Alloway was drawing nigh,
Whare ghaists and houlets nightly cry. –

By this time he was cross the ford,
Whare, in the snaw, the chapman smoor'd;
And past the birks and meikle stane,
Whare drunken Charlie brak's neck-bane;
And thro' the whins, and by the cairn,
Whare hunters fand the murder'd bairn;
And near the thorn, aboon the well,
Whare Mungo's mither hang'd hersel. –
Before him Doon pours all his floods;
The doubling storm roars thro' the woods;
The lightnings flash from pole to pole;
Near and more near the thunders roll:
When, glimmering thro' the groaning trees,
Kirk-Alloway seem'd in a bleeze;
Thro' ilka bore the beams were glancing;
And loud resounded mirth and dancing. –

Inspiring bold John Barleycorn!
What dangers thou canst make us scorn!
Wi' tippeny, we fear nae evil;
Wi' usquabae, we'll face the devil! –
The swats sae ream'd in Tammie's noddle,

Fair play, he car'd na deils a boddle.
But Maggie stood right sair astonish'd,
Till, by the heel and hand admonish'd,
She ventured forward on the light;
And, wow! Tam saw an unco sight!

Warlocks and witches in a dance;
Nae cotillion brent-new frae France,
But hornpipes, jigs, strathspeys, and reels,
Put life and mettle in their heels.
A winnock-bunker in the east,
There sat auld Nick, in shape o' beast;
A towzie tyke, black, grim, and large,
To gie them music was his charge:
He screw'd the pipes and gart them skirl,
Till roof and rafters a' did dirl. –
Coffins stood round, like open presses,
That shaw'd the dead in their last dresses;
And by some devilish cantraip slight
Each in its cauld hand held a light. –
By which heroic Tam was able
To note upon the haly table,
A murderer's banes in gibbet airns;
Twa span-lang, wee, unchristen'd bairns;
A thief, new-cutted frae a rape,
Wi' his last gasp his gab did gape;
Five tomahawks, wi' blude red-rusted;
Five scymitars, wi' murder crusted;
A garter, which a babe had strangled;
A knife, a father's throat had mangled,
Whom his ain son o' life bereft,

The grey hairs yet stack to the heft;
Wi' mair o' horrible and awefu',
Which even to name wad be unlawfu'.

As Tammie glow'rd, amaz'd, and curious,
The mirth and fun grew fast and furious:
The piper loud and louder blew;
The dancers quick and quicker flew;
They reel'd, they set, they cross'd, they cleekit,
Till ilka carlin swat and reekit,
And coost her duddies to the wark,
And linket at it in her sark!

Now, Tam, O Tam! had thae been queans,
A' plump and strapping in their teens,
Their sarks, instead o' creeshie flannen,
Been snaw-white seventeen hunder linnen!
Thir breeks o' mine, my only pair,
That ance were plush, o' gude blue hair,
I wad hae gi'en them off my hurdies,
For ae blink o' the bonie burdies!

But wither'd beldams, auld and droll,
Rigwoodie hags wad spean a foal,
Lowping and flinging on a crummock,
I wonder didna turn thy stomach.

But Tam kenn'd what was what fu' brawlie,
There was ae winsome wench and wawlie,
That night enlisted in the core,
(Lang after kenn'd on Carrick shore;

For mony a beast to dead she shot,
And perish'd mony a bony boat,
And shook baith meikle corn and bear,
And kept the country-side in fear:)
Her cutty sark, o' Paisley harn,
That while a lassie she had worn,
In longitude tho' sorely scanty,
It was her best, and she was vauntie. –
Ah! little kenn'd thy reverend grannie,
That sark she coft for her wee Nannie,
Wi' twa pund Scots, ('twas a' her riches),
Wad ever grac'd a dance of witches!

But here my Muse her wing maun cour;
Sic flights are far beyond her pow'r;
To sing how Nannie lap and flang,
(A souple jade she was, and strang),
And how Tam stood, like ane bewitch'd,
And thought his very een enrich'd;
Even Satan glowr'd, and fidg'd fu' fain,
And hotch'd an blew wi' might and main:
Till first ae caper, syne anither,
Tam tint his reason a' thegither,
And roars out, 'Weel done, Cutty-sark!'
And in an instant all was dark:
And scarcely had he Maggie rallied.
When out the hellish legion sallied.

As bees bizz out wi' angry fyke,
When plundering herds assail their byke;
As open pussie's mortal foes,

When, pop! she starts before their nose;
As eager runs the market-crowd,
When 'Catch the thief!' resounds aloud;
So Maggie runs, the witches follow,
Wi' mony an eldritch skreech and hollow.

Ah, Tam! Ah, Tam! thou'll get thy fairin!
In hell they'll roast thee like a herrin!
In vain thy Kate awaits thy comin!
Kate soon will be a woefu' woman!
Now, do thy speedy utmost, Meg,
And win the key-stane of the brig;
There at them thou thy tail may toss,
A running stream they dare na cross.
But ere the key-stane she could make,
The fient a tail she had to shake!
For Nannie, far before the rest,
Hard upon noble Maggie prest,
And flew at Tam wi' furious ettle;
But little wist she Maggie's mettle –
Ae spring brought off her master hale,
But left behind her ain gray tail:
The carlin claught her by the rump,
And left poor Maggie scarce a stump.

Now, wha this tale o' truth shall read,
Ilk man and mother's son, take heed:
Whene'er to drink you are inclin'd,
Or cutty-sarks run in your mind,
Think, ye may buy the joys o'er dear,
Remember Tam o' Shanter's mare.

BURNS NIGHT IS THE ANNUAL GET-TOGETHER WHEN THE Scots are meant to celebrate the vigour, inventiveness and sensuality of their national poet. An awful lot of them do, and as I am writing this it seems possible that Scotland might leave the United Kingdom, the better to do so. Personally, I hope it doesn't happen, because I like the variety. In Sydney I was brought up among the Scots, and in my time I sighed with longing as the girls skipped and swooped in the eightsome reel. Burns the singer, dancer and poet is a delightful symbolic figure, but he would be less interesting if he were typical. In my old days on the Edinburgh Fringe, I met several vigorous, sporran-sporting personae who thought that Burns was in their blood. He was certainly in their lungs, inducing a curdled burr whose occasional incomprehensibility gave me a private conviction that the Scots should stick with a more canonical version of the English language if at all possible.

But Burns had rhythm and musicality, and the impetus to convince you that you can never get enough of those. As if to prove to you that you indeed couldn't get enough, he made 'Tam o' Shanter' deliberately endless. But you can always pause in mid-reel, look upwards admiringly at your own flickering hand, and move a little closer to the girl in her brushed silk pink frock, as if sent by Gainsborough to explore the wild northern cities where emotions are danced and sung.

It is true only of a few great poets in English that we think of them first in terms of music. (We ought to think that of Dryden, but his couplets smothered their own lilt.) Music and dancing: everything Burns ever did was a dance, and probably still was even when he told off-colour jokes. He just lit the place up.

The diction of the poem is a wild riot of vocabulary which

even native Scotsmen might need a guide to, so Sassenachs need not feel ashamed when they occasionally can't figure out what is going on. As long as they realise that the dance hall is being torn down around their ears, they've got the message. But the occasional few lines are a lot more than mere thump and bang.

> But pleasures are like poppies spread,
> You seize the flower, its bloom is shed;
> Or like the snow falls in the river,
> A moment white – then melts for ever; . . .

Fantastic: you might say: a talent on the Keatsian level, and built for strength, to be always there.

Kubla Khan

SAMUEL TAYLOR COLERIDGE
1797

In Xanadu did Kubla Khan
   A stately pleasure-dome decree:
Where Alph, the sacred river, ran
Through caverns measureless to man
   Down to a sunless sea.

So twice five miles of fertile ground
With walls and towers were girdled round;
And there were gardens bright with sinuous rills,
Where blossomed many an incense-bearing tree;
And here were forests ancient as the hills,
Enfolding sunny spots of greenery.

But oh! that deep romantic chasm which slanted
Down the green hill athwart a cedarn cover!
A savage place! as holy and enchanted
As e'er beneath a waning moon was haunted
By woman wailing for her demon-lover!
And from this chasm, with ceaseless turmoil seething,
As if this earth in fast thick pants were breathing,
A mighty fountain momently was forced:
Amid whose swift half-intermitted burst
Huge fragments vaulted like rebounding hail,
Or chaffy grain beneath the thresher's flail:
And 'mid these dancing rocks at once and ever

It flung up momently the sacred river.
Five miles meandering with a mazy motion
Through wood and dale the sacred river ran,
Then reached the caverns measureless to man,
And sank in tumult to a lifeless ocean;
And 'mid this tumult Kubla heard from far
Ancestral voices prophesying war!

    The shadow of the dome of pleasure
    Floated midway on the waves;
    Where was heard the mingled measure
    From the fountain and the caves.
It was a miracle of rare device,
A sunny pleasure-dome with caves of ice!

    A damsel with a dulcimer
    In a vision once I saw:
    It was an Abyssinian maid
    And on her dulcimer she played,
    Singing of Mount Abora.
    Could I revive within me
    Her symphony and song,
To such a deep delight 'twould win me,
That with music loud and long,
I would build that dome in air,
That sunny dome! those caves of ice!
And all who heard should see them there,
And all should cry, Beware! Beware!
His flashing eyes, his floating hair!
Weave a circle round him thrice,
And close your eyes with holy dread

For he on honey-dew hath fed,
And drunk the milk of Paradise.

———

Coleridge's fate is to be remembered more for this poem – in whose composition he was interrupted by the Person from Porlock – than for the 'Rime of the Ancient Mariner'; and for both of those poems rather than for any share he might have had in bringing the language of English poetry back closer to the way English was actually spoken. It was a declared common aim of the Romantic poets, but here is further evidence it could not be had just by wishing. The language, after a couple of centuries of desk-bound brooding, had an irrepressible tendency to get up on stilts all by itself.

The first two lines of the poem could be said to be written in common speech, except that they go backwards. There is rarely anything poetic about putting the cart before the horse, and it is certainly a bad way to deliver the milk and eggs. Only slightly further on, the River Alph presented fewer difficulties at the time, of course, than it does now, but one would have thought that the diction throughout had a hieratic emphasis, bordering on the absurd. And I suppose the 'fast thick pants' must be much funnier now than they were then. The 'caverns measureless to man' can only mean that the caverns went on until you never got to the end of them. It sounds better than 'big caverns', but it is hardly plain speech, and reinforces one's sneaking suspicion that the Person from Porlock arrived only just in time to prevent Coleridge reaching once again for the laudanum.

Coleridge was an early victim of the notion that the juice of the poppy could make the labours of artistic creation more productive. Later on, in France, Rimbaud's bad habits suggested that there might have been something to this truly romantic idea after all. In our own time, Keith Richards of the Rolling Stones, although habitually so zonked that he could take off for dental treatment in Switzerland and go to Mexico by mistake, is living proof that a shed-load of heroin might be better for you than the mere cigarettes we thought were harmless. Even Richards, though, although he is entitled to crow ironically on the subject, would probably admit that getting off your head is a bad way to examine its contents.

The eccentric film director Ken Russell did a TV movie about the Romantic poets which looks a bit less eccentric when you actually read up on them and realise that they were pretty nutty when not applying pen to paper. David Hemmings, as Coleridge, did a lot of flinging himself about. The real Coleridge, alas, was almost certainly a bit like that. He would not have struck us as tranquil. But some of his poems were unforgettable, as this one proves. He had his unique music. 'The damsel with the dulcimer' makes us eager to forget that we don't really know where Mount Abora was. We can look it up, but we don't need to look her up. She's there, in a dream of sweetness. And then bang! The Person from Porlock arrives.

When we were students at Sydney University, one of my fellow students was a young gentleman – three-piece tweed suit, suede brogues, the works – who wrote a poem that squeezed this one into a nutshell:

> 'Weave a circle round him thrice
> And close your eyes in holy dread:

For he on buttermilk hath fed,
From New South Wales Fresh Food and Ice.'

I laughed at that for a long time. The parodist had caught the mental rhythm of his target, simultaneously fantastic and preposterous.

A fragment of The Prelude, *Book One*

WILLIAM WORDSWORTH

1798–1850

We hiss'd along the polish'd ice, in games
Confederate, imitative of the chace
And woodland pleasures, the resounding horn,
The Pack loud bellowing, and the hunted hare.
So through the darkness and the cold we flew,
And not a voice was idle; with the din,
Meanwhile, the precipices rang aloud,
The leafless trees, and every icy crag
Tinkled like iron, while the distant hills
Into the tumult sent an alien sound
Of melancholy, not unnoticed, while the stars,
Eastward, were sparkling clear, and in the west
The orange sky of evening died away.

———

A LIFETIME HAS GONE BY, AND STILL, MERCIFULLY, I HAVE
not become familiar with all of *The Prelude*. Wordsworth's long-
est poem can be measured only by the acre, but there are bits of
it that act like lyrics. In Book Eleven, the spectacular word pic-
ture where people are ice-skating on the river is not just one of
the great things in his poem, but one of the great things in all

English poetry. This is a fragment alight with the colours and textures of a winter evening.

Though a phrase like the one about the 'not unnoticed' sound of melancholy snarls with the portent of duller things to come, this fragment asks to be remembered for itself rather than as a functional part of a larger scheme. The larger scheme, alas, is to mention everything: to unload the whole panorama by the shovelful into the reader's reeling mind.

But this winter sequence, self-contained and glittering, is a small scene out of Breughel. Self-contained is precisely what Wordsworth so seldom was. His urge to cover a whole acreage with poetry – in the way that the sculptor Christo, late in the twentieth century, started wrapping up entire stretches of coast-line – could have given Wordsworth a fatal reputation for sprawl. As it is, he is still much admired. He turned against the French Revolution, as his sense of decency was bound to make him do, but his other progressive aim, to bring poetry and ordinary speech back nearer to each other, was a true revolutionary success. To my mind, however, there is a suspect quality to his torrential fluency. He is at his best when tackled in fragments.

She Walks in Beauty

LORD BYRON
1813

She walks in Beauty, like the night
Of cloudless climes and starry skies;
And all that's best of dark and bright
Meet in her aspect and her eyes:
Thus mellowed to that tender light
Which Heaven to gaudy day denies.

One shade the more, one ray the less,
Had half impaired the nameless grace
Which waves in every raven tress,
Or softly lightens o'er her face;
Where thoughts serenely sweet express,
How pure, how dear their dwelling-place.

And on that cheek, and o'er that brow,
So soft, so calm, yet eloquent,
The smiles that win, the tints that glow,
But tell of days in goodness spent,
A mind at peace with all below,
A heart whose love is innocent!

BYRON WAS AT HIS BEST AND MOST CHARACTERISTIC IN the long poem. *Childe Harold's Pilgrimage* was the sensation that made his name, and *Don Juan* was the book-length virtuoso extravaganza that sealed the deal, but anyone who doubts that Byron could have shone if confined to shorter poems should take a close look at this one and check out the perfection of its balance. 'One shade the more, one ray the less' is just a tiny example of the impetus he could keep up for pages. The only thing that makes this particular Byronic poem non-Byronic is that it is professedly to do with innocence. The innocence is at the heart of the narrator's fancied young lady, and certainly she is more innocent than Byron truly thought life or love could ever be. She might come good later – i.e., she might turn bad – but at the moment she is just a stack of iced cake, trembling in the slipstream as Byron sweeps by on his way to depravities unknown in her sweet dreams.

In real life he didn't just flirt with sin, he was actively sinful. The forbidden was a part of life, and he didn't want to leave any part of life out. The long poems *Don Juan* and *Childe Harold* are the essence of him. Leave them aside and he just sounds like a plausible crook, although he was a crook capable of writing a paean to a young woman's purity almost as if he meant it. It wasn't a matter of his being driven to long forms just because he couldn't do short ones.

In the late 1930s W. H. Auden wrote a long poem in tribute to Byron that salutes his mastery of 'the airy manner'. Auden's poem is brilliantly entertaining: a reminder that Byron was thought to be that too, although some of his contemporary references have been turned opaque by time. We should skip those and just follow the main action: he is the last poet we should allow to get bogged down in scholarship. Let his impatience be ours: he was always bursting to move on to the next love, the next war. He might have gone on fighting for liberty until hell froze over if some foreign fever hadn't finished him off. His liberty, your liberty, you name it: if he believed in a cause he would give it everything. If he felt the same way about your wife, step aside.

There was once a terrific movie about Byron. Called, confusingly, *Lady Caroline Lamb*, it was written and directed by the playwright Robert Bolt. The movie has been hard to find lately but it will probably come back, now that everything does. Sarah Miles played Lady Caroline at a pitch that left the scenery in tatters, but Richard Chamberlain, he who had been Dr Kildare, was just right for Byron if you like your romantic heroes tall, slim and impossibly handsome. (The real Byron was a bit of a lard-arse if he missed out a few too many times on swimming the Hellespont.) Laurence Olivier is in the movie, playing the Duke of Wellington with what is no doubt a thoroughly researched drawl and an arresting transposition of consonants. ('Lady Cadoline, am'n't it?') But the movie is well above being just a period romp, and so was Byron. Auden was only one of the poets who heard in Byron's headlong playfulness the very tones of the modern intelligence.

Ode on Melancholy

John Keats
1819

No, no, go not to Lethe, neither twist
   Wolf's-bane, tight-rooted, for its poisonous wine;
Nor suffer thy pale forehead to be kiss'd
   By nightshade, ruby grape of Proserpine;
     Make not your rosary of yew-berries,
   Nor let the beetle, nor the death-moth be
     Your mournful Psyche, nor the downy owl
A partner in your sorrow's mysteries;
   For shade to shade will come too drowsily,
     And drown the wakeful anguish of the soul.

But when the melancholy fit shall fall
   Sudden from heaven like a weeping cloud,
That fosters the droop-headed flowers all,
   And hides the green hill in an April shroud;
Then glut thy sorrow on a morning rose,
   Or on the rainbow of the salt sand-wave,
     Or on the wealth of globed peonies;
Or if thy mistress some rich anger shows,
   Emprison her soft hand, and let her rave,
     And feed deep, deep upon her peerless eyes.

She dwells with Beauty – Beauty that must die;
   And Joy, whose hand is ever at his lips
Bidding adieu; and aching Pleasure nigh,

Turning to poison while the bee-mouth sips:
Ay, in the very temple of Delight
Veil'd Melancholy has her sovran shrine,
Though seen of none save him whose strenuous tongue
Can burst Joy's grape against his palate fine;
His soul shall taste the sadness of her might,
And be among her cloudy trophies hung.

———

FOR KEATS, HIS ODES WERE THE TECHNICAL APEX, AND although he started another long poem, *Hyperion*, when the Odes were complete, it's permissible to suppose that he would have returned to the ode-sized format later in his career – the later career that he did not have. It is important to remember that all hints of personal doom in the Odes are merely a guess on our part. He thought he was immortal, as writers tend to do.

The opening stanza is a set of riddles and challenges that take, for the diligent reader, quite a lot of looking-up and puzzling out. It was a big risk for the poem to take, because the reader's attention might have been forfeited, but perhaps Keats already knew how he was going to start the second stanza, with a thunderclap. 'But when the melancholy fit shall fall / Sudden from heaven like a weeping cloud'. The balance and impetus of the stanza's first line are enough by themselves to prove that Keats, by this stage, could write anything. He was still subject to the occasional Miltonic inversion ('the droop-headed flowers all'), but, by and large, he was writing verse as if it were concentrated, superbly rhythmic, unforgettable prose. The 'salt sand-wave' is an arresting example of how he could compact the rhythm and release it in order to provide a rhythm beyond the rhythm: he wasn't just lyrically fluent, he could be fluent even with his hesitations.

I wanted, as a sumptuous illustration, to quote the whole of 'Ode to a Nightingale' at this point. But to do so would have been the beginning of continuing this note forever, because the appreciation of Keats can never be finished. He himself only just got started. We must not be too impressed with how he claims, in 'Ode to a Nightingale', to be half in love with easeful Death. Whenever I was in Rome, in my younger days, I would pause on the Spanish Steps, below Keats's window, and imagine him languishing there dramatically. But as the years went by and I got ever deeper into his poetry, I gave up that habit and imagined him as he must have been in his own mind, just about as alive as a man can get, full of ideas, loving the words, because he already had so much proof that they loved him.

Ideally the reader should memorise all the Odes at once, and let them jostle for position in the memory, whereupon it will be found that they all come first. As for the proper name 'Proserpine': relax if you can't say it. Keats might not have been able to say it either. He had no classical education, although he probably would have picked one up if he had lived a normal span, because he had tremendous powers of intellectual absorption. Also he was not inhibited by any fear of getting things wrong. When told that it wasn't stout Cortez, but the possibly less stout Balboa, who was silent upon a peak in Darien, Keats merely gave the shrug that means you win a few, you lose a few.

Ozymandias

1817

I met a traveller from an antique land,
Who said: Two vast and trunkless legs of stone
Stand in the desert. Near them, on the sand,
Half sunk, a shattered visage lies, whose frown
And wrinkled lip and sneer of cold command,
Tell that its sculptor well those passions read,
Which yet survive stamped on these lifeless things,
The hand that mocked them, and the heart that fed:
And on the pedestal these words appear:
'My name is Ozymandias, King of Kings:
Look on my works, ye Mighty, and despair!'
Nothing beside remains. Round the decay
Of that colossal wreck, boundless and bare
The lone and level sands stretch far away.

———

IS THIS, OR IS THIS NOT, AS GOOD AS IT SOUNDS? ONLY
the deaf would say that it is not. Sometimes the greatest critics
are the greatest fools. Mercifully, the embarrassing moment is
by now drifting back into history, when the great critic F. R.
Leavis – and he really was great, with a power of argument that
can still knock you flat – proclaimed, with echoes of *1066 and
All That*, that Shelley was not as good as Shakespeare. The

negative judgement was not entirely stupid in itself, but the suggestion that Shelley could not have developed his poetic powers further than he did was worse than an impertinence. (Shakespeare must have wandered about in his youth putting up with people saying, 'He's all right but he'll never be a Langland.') Of course Shelley would have developed further. He was full of energy: a fact proved by his continuing ability to strain your patience.

Long ago, in the nineteen sixties, an era of madness generally, I started a PhD on Shelley's debt to Dante, but my otherwise excellent supervisor refused to be convinced that there was any debt at all. Hence this book has not been written by Dr James. Possibly that was a good thing. Before my aspirations to a doctorate were finally extinguished (my supervisor had survived several years as a POW but saw no need for further suffering) I got deep enough into Shelley's poetry to realise that *Adonais*, his lament for the dead Keats, sinned only in being too long to learn. Two stanzas of it, however, got into my brain, and are still there. I think of them often as my time runs out. Shelley was prescient in guessing how that might feel. He surely had no premonition that he would manage to drown himself accidentally at the age of only twenty-nine. *Pace* Dr Leavis, if Shelley had lived he might well have gone on to be the biggest thing since Shakespeare.

LII

The One remains, the many change and pass;
Heaven's light forever shines, Earth's shadows fly;
Life, like a dome of many-colour'd glass,
Stains the white radiance of Eternity,
Until Death tramples it to fragments. – Die,

If thou wouldst be with that which thou dost seek!
Follow where all is fled! – Rome's azure sky,
Flowers, ruins, statues, music, words, are weak
The glory they transfuse with fitting truth to speak.

LIII

Why linger, why turn back, why shrink, my Heart?
Thy hopes are gone before: from all things here
They have departed; thou shouldst now depart!
A light is pass'd from the revolving year,
And man, and woman; and what still is dear
Attracts to crush, repels to make thee wither.
The soft sky smiles, the low wind whispers near:
'tis Adonais calls! oh, hasten thither,
No more let Life divide what Death can join together.

'Why linger, why turn back, why shrink, my Heart?' is a variation on the standard pentameter, which proves that Shelley, while still very young, could write the Spenserian stanza better than Spenser ever did. (Note the way that the word 'shrink' is emphasised by its positioning on the fourth beat. Most poets who have found that out are battle-weary after decades of struggle.) I recommend that the already-hooked reader should hasten thither, and marvel at the whole thing.

The Kraken

ALFRED, LORD TENNYSON
1830

Below the thunders of the upper deep,
Far, far beneath in the abysmal sea,
His ancient, dreamless, uninvaded sleep
The Kraken sleepeth: faintest sunlights flee
About his shadowy sides; above him swell
Huge sponges of millennial growth and height;
And far away into the sickly light,
From many a wondrous grot and secret cell
Unnumbered and enormous polypi
Winnow with giant arms the slumbering green.
There hath he lain for ages, and will lie
Battening upon huge sea worms in his sleep,
Until the latter fire shall heat the deep;
Then once by man and angels to be seen,
In roaring he shall rise and on the surface die.

———

THE FIRST-TIME READER OF 'THE KRAKEN' SHOULD refrain from being scornful about an archaism like 'sleepeth' before noticing that Tennyson was scientifically accurate in ascribing most of the ocean's noise and bustle to its surface and not to its depth. He had natural scientific insight, even though he managed only once to say, in his verse, that he had travelled by steam train. From his poetry you would imagine that he got around the country on a heavily accoutred horse, like King Arthur or Sir Lancelot.

The quivering, shivering reader, half-mesmerised by the stygian special effects, will notice that the grue-laden word 'grot' looks to have been dragged in to suit the decor. But the polysyllabic extravaganza of the phrase evoking the 'unnumbered and enormous polypi' falls on the metrical frame with perfect naturalness, even though 'unnumbered' is just a high-flown (or, in this case, low-flown) way of saying that there are a lot of polyps.

The impetus of the majestically doom-laden phrase devoted to the polyps propels the reader into the chilling image of their winnowing of the slumbering green, which he or she will know by now is not the cheerful village green, but the deep, dull, disgusting green that you get down there. 'Battening' makes it sound as if not even the huge sea-worms have got a chance against the Kraken. Finally up it comes, like a lunch too hastily ingested.

The poem was designed as a gut-churner, and in my case it worked. The British SF writer John Wyndham (he who invented the triffids) used the whole poem as the epigraph to his end-of-the-world novel *The Kraken Wakes*, so I had already memorised it before I got to university, and was thus able to quote Tennyson right from the beginning of my freshman year. I soon realised that a few fragments from 'Idylls of the King' were less likely to give my captive listeners the horrors, but I was dead right about Tennyson's poetry being an invitation to performance.

Certainly he thought so. I have told the story before, but I will risk telling it again, about how, after the clamorous success of his long poem 'Maud', Mrs Ruskin, politely bearding him at a crowded reception, unwisely revealed that she had not yet read it, although of course she couldn't wait. Tennyson took her at her word and recited the whole thing from memory. Having detected her occasional baffled look, he recited the whole thing again.

My Last Duchess

ROBERT BROWNING
1842

—

FERRARA

That's my last Duchess painted on the wall,
Looking as if she were alive. I call
That piece a wonder, now; Fra Pandolf's hands
Worked busily a day, and there she stands.
Will't please you sit and look at her? I said
'Fra Pandolf' by design, for never read
Strangers like you that pictured countenance,
The depth and passion of its earnest glance,
But to myself they turned (since none puts by
The curtain I have drawn for you, but I)
And seemed as they would ask me, if they durst,
How such a glance came there; so, not the first
Are you to turn and ask thus. Sir, 'twas not
Her husband's presence only, called that spot
Of joy into the Duchess' cheek; perhaps
Fra Pandolf chanced to say, 'Her mantle laps
Over my lady's wrist too much,' or 'Paint
Must never hope to reproduce the faint
Half-flush that dies along her throat.' Such stuff
Was courtesy, she thought, and cause enough
For calling up that spot of joy. She had
A heart – how shall I say? – too soon made glad,
Too easily impressed; she liked whate'er

She looked on, and her looks went everywhere.
Sir, 'twas all one! My favour at her breast,
The dropping of the daylight in the West,
The bough of cherries some officious fool
Broke in the orchard for her, the white mule
She rode with round the terrace – all and each
Would draw from her alike the approving speech,
Or blush, at least. She thanked men – good! but thanked
Somehow – I know not how – as if she ranked
My gift of a nine-hundred-years-old name
With anybody's gift. Who'd stoop to blame
This sort of trifling? Even had you skill
In speech – which I have not – to make your will
Quite clear to such an one, and say, 'Just this
Or that in you disgusts me; here you miss,
Or there exceed the mark' – and if she let
Herself be lessoned so, nor plainly set
Her wits to yours, forsooth, and made excuse –
E'en then would be some stooping; and I choose
Never to stoop. Oh, sir, she smiled, no doubt,
Whene'er I passed her; but who passed without
Much the same smile? This grew; I gave commands;
Then all smiles stopped together. There she stands
As if alive. Will't please you rise? We'll meet
The company below, then. I repeat,
The Count your master's known munificence
Is ample warrant that no just pretence
Of mine for dowry will be disallowed;
Though his fair daughter's self, as I avowed
At starting, is my object. Nay, we'll go

Together down, sir. Notice Neptune, though,
Taming a sea-horse, thought a rarity,
Which Claus of Innsbruck cast in bronze for me!

BROWNING PAINTS THE ANIMATED PICTURE OF HOW THE
Last Duchess loves everyone and the Duke hates her for it. The
Duke, who narrates, is in fact very skilled in speech, despite his
disavowal; he's just saying all the wrong things. One of the wrong
things is the strong suggestion that he has had her killed – he
'gave commands; / Then all smiles stopped together'. But the
narrator has already tipped his hand when he casually lets drop
that she was 'too soon made glad'. He is really saying, or really
not saying, that she found other men almost as attractive as him.
(I have put 'almost' in so as to cover the unlikelihood of his
admitting that she might have found other men as attractive or
even, whisper it, more attractive.)

Our narrator is a monster of the ego but well protected
against the urge to admit it. 'My gift of a nine-hundred-years-old
name' is the phrase that tips us off to his mental armour: he has
an aristocratic provenance to protect. He is no common thug.

He is, however, a thug. Our poet, a psychoanalyst before
the fact, is digging in amongst the mental tricks of the well-
connected wicked. It is easy to imagine the dramatic lay-out of
the poem being re-staged as an episode of *Columbo*, with the
narrator played by Peter Falk in a crumpled raincoat and the
Duke by Vincent Price in his silk-voiced heyday.

The dramatic monologues of Browning penetrate the mind
of the central figure. The smaller ones add up to various ways of

avoiding the indigestible immensity of *The Ring and the Book*, a maxi-epic that eventually insisted on being perpetrated, almost as if an epic could be instigated by the lyrical impulse. All the speakers in *The Ring and the Book* are equally eloquent, which unfortunately generates absurdity when the story is taken up by some lowly miscreant in bad tights.

Here we might remember that if everyone in *Much Ado About Nothing* spoke as well as Beatrice and Benedick, there would be no point in those two speaking well. As things were, Shakespeare knew how to make the ordinary people speak ordinarily. Only occasionally remembering to send on a low-life character who did not sound as if, a few minutes before, he had been setting the table on a roar in the Cafe Royal, Browning was frequently just too exuberant to rein himself in. It was a flaw inherent in his protean vitality.

All Nature Has a Feeling

JOHN CLARE
1845

All nature has a feeling: woods, fields, brooks
Are life eternal: and in silence they
Speak happiness beyond the reach of books;
There's nothing mortal in them; their decay
Is the green life of change; to pass away
And come again in blooms revivified.
Its birth was heaven, eternal is its stay,
And with the sun and moon shall still abide
Beneath their day and night and heaven wide.

———◆———

WHEN IT COMES TO JOHN CLARE, THE HARD WORK consists mainly in struggling not to drown in the detail he has revealed to you. Blessed, or cursed, with the knack for omnidirectional attention, he notices everything, especially about life in the countryside; but no reader's attention can survive noticing everything at once. While the poet revels in the rustic detail, the reader curses the abiding fact that he himself was not born to the green wellingtons, the oiled Barbour and the bouncing Land Rover.

A spare elegance is hard to find in Clare. He's more crowded than any old barn. But this is one poem which seems to me to have benefited from a sudden determination on his part, perhaps while lying awake, to write a more austere poem the next day. Clare had it all: and almost always he overcrowds the poem in the attempt to prove that. But for once he relaxes, and the reader can do the same.

We should not forget, by the way, to scan 'heaven' as a single syllable. Such was the convention from the very start of English poetry all the way through into the twentieth century. There was a time when the elision would be usefully marked, but more often it was just left without a sign-post, seemingly in order to ensure that all who came across it could come a-cropper. Nowadays the green life of change has revivified the bloom, so that uninstructed readers, when they encounter the word 'heaven', are less likely to make mincemeat of the metre.

Remember

CHRISTINA ROSSETTI
1849

Remember me when I am gone away,
   Gone far away into the silent land;
   When you can no more hold me by the hand,
Nor I half turn to go yet turning stay.
Remember me when no more day by day
   You tell me of our future that you plann'd:
   Only remember me; you understand
It will be late to counsel then or pray.
Yet if you should forget me for a while
   And afterwards remember, do not grieve:
   For if the darkness and corruption leave
   A vestige of the thoughts that once I had,
Better by far you should forget and smile
   Than that you should remember and be sad.

―――

CHRISTINA ROSSETTI COULD BE UNEVEN WITHIN THE space of a few lines, but she had a lyrical impetus that held a poem together even as it shook in the eddies of her variably precise language. If you doubt the pervasiveness of that drawback, take another look at the first line. Where else could she be gone except 'away'?

Yet rhyming with that dubious coup, and only three lines into the future, is 'Nor I half turn to go and turning stay', which is perfectly dramatic, and governs, with its echo, the swaying back-and-forth progression of the rest of the poem. It's like a hesitation waltz: lovely when it flows, and lovelier still when it seems to falter.

At least in her mind, Christina Rossetti was a bit of an after-dinner performer. After the tricky turn by which she goes and stays, she stays to begin a long exit. The line 'Yet if you should forget me for a while' really means 'forget me and my ghost will return to make a shambles of your sock drawer' but she's got it covered by saying, with what sounds almost exactly like sincerity, that she would rather he failed to remember than that he should be depressed.

Even if she is only pretending to mean that, however, the question of why she wrote the poem at all would be enough to conjure a haunting answer: if she leaves him with a sufficiently taxing puzzle to solve, he might go on thinking of her in perpetuity, however long that might prove to be. If we tell someone to forget us, are we really content to be forgotten?

How do I love thee?

ELIZABETH BARRETT BROWNING
1850

How do I love thee? Let me count the ways.
I love thee to the depth and breadth and height
My soul can reach, when feeling out of sight
For the ends of being and ideal grace.
I love thee to the level of every day's
Most quiet need, by sun and candle-light.
I love thee freely, as men strive for right;
I love thee purely, as they turn from praise.
I love thee with the passion put to use
In my old griefs, and with my childhood's faith.
I love thee with a love I seemed to lose
With my lost saints. I love thee with the breath,
Smiles, tears, of all my life; and, if God choose,
I shall but love thee better after death.

———◆———

I FOUND HER HUSBAND ROBERT BROWNING FIRST AND HE
was clearly a genius, and at that time I thought of Elizabeth
Barrett Browning as being in his shadow. Later on I realised that
in fact she was the cure for his blaze of light: a sensible element;
a passionate moderation. This is a poem about continual discov-
ery, and embodies the thrill so well that it can be continually
rediscovered. Today I look for a line or phrase in this poem to

focus on and 'when feeling out of sight / For the ends of being and ideal grace' comes shining out. Here, in her quiet way, she's abandoning her sense of proportion. Excess, at this point, must be the only appropriate level of language, even if we don't exactly know whether her great love lies there dying or is about to come bounding in with a stack of pastries from the nearby cake shop. Or maybe she's the one that's dying.

Reading around in the biographical material might give us a more precise idea of the circumstances, but what matters here is that she doesn't. Everything that's actually happening is left out. There is only the registration of a mood, and the mood is exaltation mixed with desperation. It's the best thing life can offer, now that God is out of the picture.

He almost is; He is deputed to do the choosing at the end, but His saints have already gone; they were figments of her childhood's faith, and now she no longer believes all that. Or rather, she no longer believes most of that. Yet there is still a manifestation of the divine for her to have faith in. There's this chap, and how she loves him. How much? Tell him again.

Dover Beach

MATTHEW ARNOLD
1851

The sea is calm tonight.
The tide is full, the moon lies fair
Upon the straits; on the French coast the light
Gleams and is gone; the cliffs of England stand,
Glimmering and vast, out in the tranquil bay.
Come to the window, sweet is the night-air!
Only, from the long line of spray
Where the sea meets the moon-blanched land,
Listen! you hear the grating roar
Of pebbles which the waves draw back, and fling,
At their return, up the high strand,
Begin, and cease, and then again begin,
With tremulous cadence slow, and bring
The eternal note of sadness in.

Sophocles long ago
Heard it on the Ægean, and it brought
Into his mind the turbid ebb and flow
Of human misery; we
Find also in the sound a thought,
Hearing it by this distant northern sea.

The Sea of Faith
Was once, too, at the full, and round earth's shore
Lay like the folds of a bright girdle furled.

But now I only hear
Its melancholy, long, withdrawing roar,
Retreating, to the breath
Of the night-wind, down the vast edges drear
And naked shingles of the world.

Ah, love, let us be true
To one another! for the world, which seems
To lie before us like a land of dreams,
So various, so beautiful, so new,
Hath really neither joy, nor love, nor light,
Nor certitude, nor peace, nor help for pain;
And we are here as on a darkling plain
Swept with confused alarms of struggle and flight,
Where ignorant armies clash by night.

—————

JUST BECAUSE MATTHEW ARNOLD WROTE WHAT IS POSSIBLY
the least quotable line in all English poetry ('Who prop, thou
ask'st, in these bad days, my mind?') is no reason to ignore a
creation like 'Dover Beach', which is so rhythmic throughout
that it starts teaching itself to you at first reading. Nor is it over-
laden with classical furniture, although Sophocles, when he gets
into the poem, makes you wonder whether he will be sticking
around for long.

Luckily the action stays focused on the sheltering couple
looking at the seashore. A long time later, Keith Douglas cap-
tured the same tone and the same situation in his pre-WWII
poem 'Canoe'. The similarities of tone are striking, although in

fact Arnold, in no physical danger, was only likely to run the risks of complacency. To get really excited about him, you have to take in his full range, not just as a poet, but as a critic and commentator on culture.

In a poem full of great ideas, the greatest is the 'melancholy, long, withdrawing roar' – the retreat of religious faith from history. It was a huge fact and a great challenge. What would replace it? Arnold suggested that Love might do the trick, but how has that turned out? In our time, the inevitable suggestion is that the replacement might be art itself. Note, by the way, that there is a very funny parody of 'Dover Beach' by Anthony Hecht.

From The Rubaiyat of Omar Khayyam

Translated by Edward Fitzgerald
1859

I

Wake! For the Sun, who scatter'd into flight
The Stars before him from the Field of Night,
Drives Night along with them from Heav'n, and strikes
The Sultan's Turret with a Shaft of Light.

VII

Come, fill the Cup, and in the fire of Spring
Your Winter-garment of Repentance fling:
The Bird of Time has but a little way
To flutter – and the Bird is on the Wing.

XII

A Book of Verses underneath the Bough,
A Jug of Wine, a Loaf of Bread, and Thou
Beside me singing in the Wilderness –
Oh, Wilderness were Paradise enow!

XVII

Think, in this batter'd Caravanserai
Whose Portals are alternate Night and Day,
How Sultan after Sultan with his Pomp
Abode his destined Hour, and went his way.

XIX

I sometimes think that never blows so red
The Rose as where some buried Caesar bled;
That every Hyacinth the Garden wears
Dropt in her Lap from some once lovely Head.

LXXI

The Moving Finger writes; and, having writ,
Moves on: nor all thy Piety nor Wit
Shall lure it back to cancel half a Line,
Nor all thy Tears wash out a Word of it.

——

IN 1859 EDWARD FITZGERALD PUBLISHED HIS TRANSLATION of Persian quatrains attributed to the eleventh-century poet Omar Khayyam. It's fabulous stuff, but even in the days when it was a standard recital piece in every genteel English household, few dreamed of performing the whole thing. They wanted to provide a suggestion of its eternal elements. Everyone had their favourite bits. These are some of mine, and by no coincidence I inherited them from my mother.

My mother used to read the *Rubaiyat* to me. She was not a literary person, and this was when I was very small. She always observed the rhythm very carefully. In the great line 'Nor all thy Tears wash out a Word of it' she was careful to put the emphasis on the word 'tears' – an emphasis that sums up the rhythmic process of the whole stanza, and indeed of the whole poem. I wish now that I had paid more attention. I must have been rather a stupid child. I had to find it all out for myself again, later on.

Robert Graves thought he'd done a superior version of the *Rubaiyat*, but unfortunately he left out the rhythm, the imagery and almost every other element of interest. One can imagine his companion Laura Riding (whose strategy for winning an argument with Graves was to throw herself backwards out of a high window) nodding in approval.

The *Rubaiyat* is one of those exotic works of art that have the gift of retaining their fascination even when they become a busted flush. Many years later the great literary satirist S. J. Perelman could be sure of his effect when he invented the line 'And thou beside me, yacketing in the wilderness.' The gag works because the underlying atmosphere of tranquillity is still strong.

The Dalliance of the Eagles

WALT WHITMAN
1880

Skirting the river road, (my forenoon walk, my rest,)
Skyward in air a sudden muffled sound, the dalliance of the eagles,
The rushing amorous contact high in space together,
The clinching interlocking claws, a living, fierce, gyrating wheel,
Four beating wings, two beaks, a swirling mass tight grappling,
In tumbling turning clustering loops, straight downward falling,
Till o'er the river pois'd, the twain yet one, a moment's lull,
A motionless still balance in the air, then parting, talons loosing,
Upward again on slow-firm pinions slanting, their
    separate diverse flight,
She hers, he his, pursuing.

———

THIS IS A RARE EXAMPLE OF POETRY BY WALT WHITMAN
that actually sounds like poetry. He also wrote the longest poem
in the world that doesn't really sound like poetry even for thirty
seconds, yet somehow it is: a great mystery. Most of *Leaves of
Grass* is not only arrhythmic but anti-rhythmic; so unlike poetry
that it isn't like prose either. You can break your jaw trying to
recite it. Everyone can quote, possibly with a few judicious eli-
sions, the bit about 'I believe a leaf of grass is no less than the
journeywork of the stars.' What the bedazzled reciters seldom
admit is that they find very few passages to equal it for sayability.

But memorability, at least in Whitman's case, is another thing. He gets into your system like an injection of vitamins. The secret of his magic powers of incantation can be readily detected in 'The Dalliance of the Eagles'.

'A swirling mass tight grappling.' Physical love is like that for human beings. Whitman finds no room to say, in this poem, and in fact found little room to say anywhere, that physical love for him was a same-sex phenomenon, but nobody sane, even in those days, could have been in any doubt that Whitman was homosexual. One of the many remarkable things about him is that he lived out his life without being jailed or lynched. The life, however, was tough enough: as a hospital orderly he saw the very worst of the Civil War, and the man who ended up wearing nothing but a hat as he stood beside the pond and contemplated the evanescence of life had seen far more than his share of lingering death.

Yet everything he wrote was full of life, even when it stumbled awkwardly. Randall Jarrell wrote a great thing about Whitman: quoting a particularly awkward passage from *Leaves of Grass*, he said it was 'really *ingeniously* bad'. The hidden suggestion in Jarrell's appreciation was that Whitman planned it all. It might have been so. Certainly Whitman has lasted well. There are American poets even more torrentially productive that we no longer read, but Whitman is already there forever, as it were. The first impression you get from his work might even be the last impression that you take with you: that life is really like this: a vivid sprawl, a sumptuous chaos.

There is more than enough by Whitman himself to keep any reader going for years, but one little book about him can be heavily recommended. Galway Kinnell edited a short selection. Since Kinnell himself was the author of an American epic that undoubtedly worked (*The Avenue Bearing the Initial of Christ into the New World*), his qualifications for praising Whitman were impeccable. And Kinnell knew a lot about poetic form, so his disinclination to find Whitman poetically formless is a powerful hint that we might be in the presence of something unique.

Spring

GERARD MANLEY HOPKINS
1877

Nothing is so beautiful as Spring –
   When weeds, in wheels, shoot long and lovely and lush;
   Thrush's eggs look little low heavens, and thrush
Through the echoing timber does so rinse and wring
The ear, it strikes like lightnings to hear him sing;
   The glassy peartree leaves and blooms, they brush
   The descending blue; that blue is all in a rush
With richness; the racing lambs too have fair their fling.

What is all this juice and all this joy?
   A strain of the earth's sweet being in the beginning
In Eden garden. – Have, get, before it cloy,
   Before it cloud, Christ, lord, and sour with sinning,
Innocent mind and Mayday in girl and boy,
   Most, O maid's child, thy choice and worthy the winning.

———◆———

IN THIS QUIRKILY COMPULSIVE MASTERPIECE BY GERARD
Manley Hopkins, the phrase 'little low heavens' is the true start
of the poem. Until then it's all warm-up, and even sounds stan-
dard, not to say staid. But the little low heavens are beyond
metaphorical. They constitute a sudden upgrading of the world
view. Finding such things and being overwhelmed by them is

the big game of poetry. The very occasional poet like Hopkins seems out to remind us that poetry isn't just words: it's visions. And the question is, often, visions of where?

Well, heaven. It's in the poem. He looks at the bird's eggs and sees paradise on Earth. The rest of us might look at them and see lunch, but Hopkins is on a different plane. Surely his idiosyncratic diction is meant to remind us of that: of monkishly austere dedication, those head-banging moments of spiritual revelation in the tight-fitting cell.

His mentor Robert Bridges wanted to straighten his quirks out so as to make him more marketably normal, i.e. more like Robert Bridges. Somehow Hopkins got his body of work done despite offers of help. In my time there were still prominent critics who couldn't abide his quirks, but the long run did its work and nowadays it takes a dolt to question his achievement. The flaring moments are too brilliant to be blinked away. 'The racing lambs have fair their fling.' Why are they jumping backwards? you ask. But come on, haven't you ever seen lambs racing? They bounce around.

Hopkins took delight in life. 'What is all this juice and all this joy?' For him, the whole world was Eden garden. In his great long poem 'The Wreck of the Deutschland', the drowning passengers are leaving here more than they are arriving there. Praise him.

There's a certain Slant of Light

EMILY DICKINSON
1890

There's a certain Slant of light,
Winter Afternoons –
That oppresses, like the Heft
Of Cathedral Tunes –

Heavenly Hurt, it gives us –
We can find no scar,
But internal difference –
Where the Meanings, are –

None may teach it – Any –
'Tis the seal Despair –
An imperial affliction
Sent us of the Air –

When it comes, the Landscape listens –
Shadows – hold their breath –
When it goes, 'tis like the Distance
On the look of Death –

I HAVE TO CONFESS TO HAVING MIXED FEELINGS ABOUT Emily Dickinson – the kind of confession that in America can lead to you being locked up. In her homeland, no one is allowed to be less than worshipful of her miniaturised density. There are reasons for worshipping her, and the reasons are better than for worshipping, say, an Aztec priest – but the cold truth is that you wish most of her poems were like longer poems instead of short notes. (You look at one of her poems and think, 'Yes, she could probably have made a good poem out of that.') But in spite of my conviction that she always said just that crucial bit too little, I have always had the urge to read more of her. Her collected works are a bowl of beads. In her life she was dedicated and self-sacrificing but those qualities on their own aren't necessarily poetic. Poetic qualities, on the other hand, are. Any amount of posthumous psychiatric analysis directed at her eccentric personality can't take away the central stability of her strange magic. Shadows still hold their breath when she speaks.

Non sum qualis eram bonae sub regno Cynarae

By Ernest Dowson

1894

Last night, ah, yesternight, betwixt her lips and mine,
There fell thy shadow, Cynara! thy breath was shed
Upon my soul between the kisses and the wine;
And I was desolate and sick of an old passion,
    Yea, I was desolate and bowed my head:
I have been faithful to thee, Cynara! in my fashion.

All night upon my heart I felt her warm heart beat,
Night-long within my arms in love and sleep she lay;
Surely the kisses of her bought red mouth were sweet;
But I was desolate and sick of an old passion,
    When I awoke and found the dawn was grey:
I have been faithful to thee, Cynara! in my fashion.

I have forgot much, Cynara! gone with the wind,
Flung roses, roses riotously with the throng,
Dancing, to put thy pale, lost lilies out of mind;
But I was desolate and sick of an old passion,
    Yea, all the time, because the dance was long:
I have been faithful to thee, Cynara! in my fashion.

I cried for madder music and for stronger wine,
But when the feast is finished and the lamps expire,
Then falls thy shadow, Cynara! the night is thine;

And I am desolate and sick of an old passion,
　　Yea, hungry for the lips of my desire:
I have been faithful to thee, Cynara! in my fashion.

———————

ERNEST DOWSON WAS OFTEN KEEN TO GET HIS LATEST poem up on stilts by giving it a Latin title, no doubt riveting the attention of any Roman legionaries who happened to be idling nearby. The title of this poem means 'I'm not what I was under the reign of the good Cynara'. He is on the couch with a courtesan, yet it is Cynara who still has his heart. Whether Cynara was a courtesan too is open to question. One suspects that she might have been, since the poem is so keen to exhale an atmosphere of classical decadence.

The diction of the poem is antique armour. Unfortunately it works against the reader, who is slowed down in penetrating to the core of the poem's meaning and might give up altogether. But once you get there, you get to the nub of an almost universal (one daringly assumes) human experience. You might indeed lie there in somebody's strong toils of grace and be thinking of somebody else.

In addition to its deeper-than-you-suspected psychological complexity, the poem is richly laden with memorable cadences. Try forgetting the 'bought red mouth' of the prostitute. Most famous of the poem's sugar-dusted phrases is 'gone with the wind', a stroke of genius borrowed by Margaret Mitchell as the title for her famous novel. 'I cried for madder music and for stronger wine' was a line often cried out by the supposedly mature Clive James in the days when he was under the table after two drinks.

When I was a student in Sydney there was a downtown professional production of *Long Day's Journey into Night*, starring the great Muriel Steinbeck as Eugene O'Neill's junkie mother. I loved it all but was particularly gripped by the way that the two young men recited Dowson's poems to each other. I went away afterwards remembering the poems more than O'Neill's dialogue. Poetry often gets to you by an unexpected route.

T. S. Eliot called Dowson the most gifted and technically perfect poet of his age. It seems like an extravagant claim, until you try to get one of Dowson's poems out of your head. You might forget the bits in Latin (only the occasional berserk scholar thinks he knows how to pronounce Cynara) but everything in English tends to linger like incense fumes.

Cargoes

JOHN MASEFIELD
1903

Quinquireme of Nineveh from distant Ophir,
Rowing home to haven in sunny Palestine,
With a cargo of ivory,
And apes and peacocks,
Sandalwood, cedarwood, and sweet white wine.

Stately Spanish galleon coming from the Isthmus,
Dipping through the Tropics by the palm-green shores,
With a cargo of diamonds,
Emeralds, amethysts,
Topazes, and cinnamon, and gold moidores.

Dirty British coaster with a salt-caked smoke stack,
Butting through the Channel in the mad March days,
With a cargo of Tyne coal,
Road-rails, pig-lead,
Firewood, iron-ware, and cheap tin trays.

———

WHEN I WAS AT SCHOOL IN SYDNEY, JOHN MASEFIELD WAS
still Poet Laureate, and therefore famous throughout the Empire,
as it still then was. But he wasn't famous for any poems written
about the Royal Family, who were nominally his employers, he

was famous for this poem, which a whole generation of suffering schoolchildren were compelled to learn by heart. Most of them didn't get any further than the first word, which probably needs to be looked up even now. (It's a ship with five banks of oars, but you've guessed that.) For 'Nineveh' you might need a map, or else find all you need to know on Google. The same applies to 'Ophir', and so on. The poem is full of place-names and exotic things.

The progression of the narrative, from the first stanza to the third and last, is the story of the names and things becoming less exotic as they get closer to home, until finally they end up surrounding us. It's a brilliant idea – progression through declension – but it would have been much less interesting if Masefield had not been such a master of verbal music. He knew how to set the syllables chiming as if they were the silver leaves of a vibraharp. 'With a cargo of diamonds, / Emeralds, amethysts': he gets music into the turning of a line, although a bit later the reader might be googling again, to get the precise meaning of 'moidores'.

The poem finally comes to earth, as it were, when the quinquireme, and its successor the Spanish galleon, are transmogrified into the dirty British coaster. The world is plural, changeable, malleable, but the ships are eternal. (We might remember here that he wasn't out of date so much as prescient. Masefield had lived long enough to see ships challenged for supremacy by aircraft, but in fact the ships are still here, although he might have found a deck-load of containers a less evocative cargo.)

The Poet Laureate, whoever he or she is at the time, tends to be in a vulnerable position, because of the sometimes ungainly postures he or she must adopt in order to write about royal news, or sometimes more importantly, not write about it. But even though it's got the air of a useful theme having been deliberately chosen and mechanically adhered to, this poem is a training ship for poets. I still find it rollickingly speakable. There is the hint of a debt to Swinburne – Swinburne when he is being rhythmically over-ripe, and too lushly poetic – but there is a redeeming specificity to the images, as if Masefield really knows how the ships differ from each other, and might have been personally involved in cinnamon futures or sandalwood exchange.

Harp Song of the Dane Women

RUDYARD KIPLING

1906

What is a woman that you forsake her,
And the hearth-fire and the home-acre,
To go with the old grey Widow-maker?

She has no house to lay a guest in –
But one chill bed for all to rest in,
That the pale suns and the stray bergs nest in.

She has no strong white arms to fold you,
But the ten-times-fingering weed to hold you –
Out on the rocks where the tide has rolled you.

Yet, when the signs of summer thicken,
And the ice breaks, and the birch-buds quicken,
Yearly you turn from our side, and sicken –

Sicken again for the shouts and the slaughters.
You steal away to the lapping waters,
And look at your ship in her winter-quarters.

You forget our mirth, and talk at the tables,
The kine in the shed and the horse in the stables –
To pitch her sides and go over her cables.

Then you drive out where the storm-clouds swallow,
And the sound of your oar-blades, falling hollow,
Is all we have left through the months to follow.

Ah, what is Woman that you forsake her,
And the hearth-fire and the home-acre,
To go with the old grey Widow-maker?

———

IT'S NOTHING LIKE THE REST OF KIPLING'S POETRY
because it has no English soldiers speaking the vernacular.
There's no Cockney in it, and yet the rhythm, once you have
taken in its rolling tread, can only be him. In fact he was setting
the standards for years to come, perhaps still for now. Such was
his rhythmic control that he could set a pattern and make a
coup, an effect, from breaking out of it. In the triplet that starts
'What is a woman that you forsake her?', the next phrases, 'And
the hearth-fire' and 'and the home-acre' are both deliberately out
of tempo, and they both contribute to making the overall tempo
even more forceful.

For some reason the poem always reminds me irresistibly of
the awesome athleticism of Kirk Douglas dancing on the oars of
his longship in the film *The Vikings*, although Kipling probably
had a less off-putting grin of satisfaction. There is almost always
joy in virtuosity. And the vigour of this poem makes you almost
glad that people conquered each other, so that Kipling could
write about them. But only almost. If anyone was sensitive to the
horrors of war it was Kipling, who lost his son in the First World
War, and never got over it, except by getting on with writing a

whole library full of wonderful stuff. His *Captains Courageous* was the first great book I ever read, and it was so thrilling I didn't even realise it was literature.

From Lepanto

G. K. CHESTERTON

1911

White founts falling in the courts of the sun,
And the Soldan of Byzantium is smiling as they run;
There is laughter like the fountains in that face of all men feared,
It stirs the forest darkness, the darkness of his beard,
It curls the blood-red crescent, the crescent of his lips,
For the inmost sea of all the earth is shaken with his ships.
They have dared the white republics up the capes of Italy,
They have dashed the Adriatic round the Lion of the Sea,
And the Pope has cast his arms abroad for agony and loss,
And called the kings of Christendom for swords about the Cross,
The cold queen of England is looking in the glass;
The shadow of the Valois is yawning at the Mass;
From evening isles fantastical rings faint the Spanish gun,
And the Lord upon the Golden Horn is laughing in the sun.

Dim drums throbbing, in the hills half heard,
Where only on a nameless throne a crownless prince has stirred,
Where, risen from a doubtful seat and half attainted stall,
The last knight of Europe takes weapons from the wall,
The last and lingering troubadour to whom the bird has sung,
That once went singing southward when all the world was young,
In that enormous silence, tiny and unafraid,
Comes up along a winding road the noise of the Crusade.
Strong gongs groaning as the guns boom far,
Don John of Austria is going to the war,

Stiff flags straining in the night-blasts cold
In the gloom black-purple, in the glint old-gold,
Torchlight crimson on the copper kettle-drums,
Then the tuckets, then the trumpets, then the cannon, and he comes.
Don John laughing in the brave beard curled,
Spurning of his stirrups like the thrones of all the world,
Holding his head up for a flag of all the free.
Love-light of Spain – hurrah!
Death-light of Africa!
Don John of Austria
Is riding to the sea.

———

ONCE UPON A TIME G. K. CHESTERTON WAS THE MOST
famous journalist in the English-speaking world, and now he
isn't: a warning to any current journalist who fancies himself
indispensable. But Chesterton was so brilliant that he had a lot
of sparkle left over after writing a couple of columns a day. He
wrote several excellent critical monographs – the one on
Dickens can particularly be recommended – and on top of his
criticism he wrote poetry worth criticising.

'Lepanto', indeed, is more than just a party piece, although
when you first hear it recited at a public gathering you might
think it had been designed purely as text for virtuoso verbal
performers. The tip-off to its show-business ambitions is the
recurring line about Don John of Austria, who in the course of
the poem's long narrative sweep is variously characterised as
going to the war, coming back from the war, or adopting various
other military postures. The poem is far too long to be quoted

holus-bolus here, but I have broken the rule of quoting things only entire, because this poem was always a collection of vignettes. You can break back into it anywhere, and it will always start again.

'Lepanto' has a tremendous impetus, mainly based on Chesterton's gift for rhythm. He had that in his prose too, but people tended not to notice. In poetry, rhythm looks like a gift, whereas in prose, it tends not to be noticed except when you realise that those prose writers without it are exhausting to read, particularly if you are reading them aloud. Reading aloud ought not to be a lost art, and nowadays we suffer from the fact that nobody at the party is likely to stand up beside the piano and evoke the equivalent of Don John of Austria. 'Dim drums throbbing, in the hills half heard . . .' I picked that line more or less at random, feeling safe because almost every line of the poem is like that. Chesterton really did have a gift as big as his famous tummy, which entered the room before he did.

In Death Divided

Thomas Hardy

1912

I

I shall rot here, with those whom in their day
    You never knew,
And alien ones who, ere they chilled to clay,
    Met not my view,
Will in your distant grave-place ever neighbour you.

II

No shade of pinnacle or tree or tower,
    While earth endures,
Will fall on my mound and within the hour
    Steal on to yours;
One robin never haunt our two green covertures.

III

Some organ may resound on Sunday noons
    By where you lie,
Some other thrill the panes with other tunes
    Where moulder I;
No selfsame chords compose our common lullaby.

IV

The simply-cut memorial at my head
    Perhaps may take
A Gothic form, and that above your bed

Be Greek in make;
No linking symbol show thereon for our tale's sake.

V

And in the monotonous moils of strained, hard-run
    Humanity,
The eternal tie which binds us twain in one
    No eye will see
Stretching across the miles that sever you from me.

—

BACK IN SYDNEY IN THE LATE 1950S, I WOULD APPOINT myself guardian of the radiogram at parties, and make sure I was the one who chose the next track on the Caedmon album of recited poems. My most favoured reciter was Dylan Thomas, and among his recitals the one I was most thrilled by was his rendition of this poem by Hardy. I call it a rendition because there was a distinct musical element: Dylan Thomas elevated his voice to meet the challenge and turned the poem into a succession of moments so that it sounded as gorgeous as possible, rather like a great actress at the height of her beauty preening before the wrap-around mirror – if that doesn't sound too visual an evocation of what was essentially a sonic event. His voice was wonderful, totally making you forget that in real life he looked like a spiteful potato whose chief aim was to borrow your money (no, wait a second: his chief aim was not to pay it back). Anyway, Dylan Thomas would stop the show with this one. That last line still stops my breath.

On the other hand, I think that the 'monotonous moils' is one of the many instances in Hardy of the poet over-egging the pudding. It is seldom admitted now that Hardy as a poet was almost too mannered to be put up with. Mainly because Philip Larkin favoured him, Hardy is often thought to be his predecessor in the art of plain speech, but in fact Hardy was more baroque than a baldacchino by Bernini. Thomas's magnificent voice had the effect of straightening out Hardy's elaborate diction into something that sounded like plain English – or, if you like, plain Welsh English. All the more effective, then, when the Welsh bard piled on the sonority. I still shiver to the way Thomas made the last line of Hardy's poem soar away into the distance like a bird of prey taking off into the dawn.

As so often in Hardy's verse, half the lines in this poem are written backwards. He was very fond, in fact, of the contrived scenario, as in the poem about the *Titanic* and the iceberg, in which the iceberg emerges as the protagonist. Hardy was continually flogging meaning into poetic situations that already possessed meaning. A case of overloading the circuits.

The seemingly paradoxical truth about Hardy as a poet was that he started off as if he had everything it took but continued as if he needed to strain for effect. In his poem 'The Voice', he could use an unforgettable phrase such as 'air-blue gown' and not realise that he didn't have to back it up with extravagant syntactical tricks and strained rhymes. He was a professional striving hopelessly for amateur status.

In a Station of the Metro

EZRA POUND

1913

The apparition of these faces in the crowd:
Petals on a wet, black bough.

———

PERMISSIBLE JOKES ABOUT EZRA POUND MAY OFTEN turn on the fact that he translated a lot of Chinese verse without being able to read Chinese. Among other poets, a Pound-foolish worshipper like Christopher Logue took courage from such facts to translate Homer. Logue's translation, *War Music*, still stands up well, but to see what a translation really can do, the reader should look at what Fitzgerald did with the *Rubaiyat* of Omar Khayyam.

The two lines quoted at the head of this chapter constitute the Ezra Pound poem that everyone remembers, perhaps because it can be learned in ten seconds. When you first read it, it's exciting for several reasons. Though 'apparition' is possibly a dispensable word, otherwise it's as spare as a hare's collar bone. (Yeats himself was flirting with the concept of the mini-poem when he wrote that phrase.) Pound's couplet-sized poem is on the other end of the scale of magnitude from, say, *Paradise Lost*, and also draws upon your own first memories of the Paris Métro. (Remember the day when you got off the train at Châtelet and thought you might be downstairs from the Louvre, and then you worked out, to your shame, with that cup of coffee over which you met the mysterious stranger who ever since has shared your life, that you were in the wrong spot except that you were in the right one, *mais certainement*?)

Nobody feels like that about the London tube system, and as for the New York subway, it might have been designed from the beginning to destroy any notion of public elegance. Pound was on to something about presenting a single image as a complete poem, but there were limits to that ambition, and they were almost instantly reached. Where could the approach go next? One of the first places it went was into slightly longer micro-poems, such as:

> And the days are not full enough
> And the nights are not full enough
> And life slips by like a field mouse
> > Not shaking the grass

But already the reader is involved in practical questions such as: exactly how much does a field mouse not shake the grass? Doesn't it shake the grass a tiny bit? The true setting for Pound's concept of the micro-poem was as a component in his *Cantos*, which went on for ever using micro-poems as 'points of light' – the micro-poetic phrase invented by Peggy Noonan in a doomed attempt to make George Bush Sr's limping speeches vivid. Nobody would have forgotten it if only he could have remembered it.

But when it comes to the Métro station poem, it's not the poem I don't like; it's Pound himself. In my early enthusiasm for his work (and I really was, in the strict sense, crazy about it, especially when it was making allusions to languages I couldn't read and he couldn't either) I knew little about his politics and I severely underestimated the extent that he was a foaming headcase. Luckily my natural propensities and aversions, aided perhaps by at least a modicum of reading contemporary historical prose written by people capable of writing about Mussolini without bringing in versified information about the bronzesmelting techniques of the Han dynasty, eventually took over from my misplaced admiration for the *uomo universale* from Idaho. By a disposition of soul, I've just got this weird, irrational aversion to screaming Fascists. Pound was the kind of Fascist who would urge his adopted government to get on with the task of wiping out his enemies. Therefore I declare that my abiding admiration for these few neatly linked words is an act of generosity on my part, as it was undoubtedly an indication of a talented eye and ear on his.

The idea of the epic in miniature proved artistically fatal when he came to attempt writing an epic at full scale. *The Cantos* are, or is, studded throughout with imagist moments which are meant to hold the magic ship together like golden nails, but in fact they just let in the water.

> To build the city of Dioce whose terraces are the colour
> of stars

It's one of the key moments in *The Cantos*. Unfortunately it's got 'key moment' written all over it. We should watch out for the single unforgettable image that gets into the mind and refuses to fade. On television once, Stacy Keach (was it?) walked towards the camera quoting Pound to this effect: 'The unbearable tragedy of the dream / in the peasant's bent shoulders'. I personally know one viewer who never forgot that moment of poetry, but for that very reason it took her a little while to catch up with the fact that by the Dream (always with a capital 'D') Pound meant Mussolini's Fascist imperium. Even after he was locked up for the stretch of imprisonment that saved him from the gallows, Pound himself was very slow to deduce that the Dream was a farcical nightmare. Poets simply can't afford to gamble everything on a single turn of phrase, and neither can their readers.

The Soldier

RUPERT BROOKE

1914

If I should die, think only this of me:
    That there's some corner of a foreign field
That is for ever England. There shall be
    In that rich earth a richer dust concealed;
A dust whom England bore, shaped, made aware,
    Gave, once, her flowers to love, her ways to roam;
A body of England's, breathing English air,
    Washed by the rivers, blest by suns of home.

And think, this heart, all evil shed away,
    A pulse in the eternal mind, no less
    Gives somewhere back the thoughts by England given;
Her sights and sounds; dreams happy as her day;
    And laughter, learnt of friends; and gentleness,
        In hearts at peace, under an English heaven.

———

RUPERT BROOKE'S REPUTATION NEVER RECOVERED FROM his popularity. The popularity included his being a darling of the upper classes. In fact he started off in the aspiring middle class, but his brains took him upwards, and his godlike good looks ensured that he would fit in when he arrived. Even after his death, he was thought to be so privileged that he had not been killed in the war at all. He had been. But he was killed a long way from France and England; and killed not by a bullet, but by a bug. He died of blood-poisoning on a hospital ship in the Aegean, while waiting to land at Gallipoli. He never got to the battle, and he never quite got to the respectable immortality of the dead British war poets either: sepsis didn't count.

Brooke is still well known for having written a poem about Grantchester, but the poem itself has rather faded. The last stanza is by now its main claim to fame, and of that only the last line is really remembered: 'And is there honey still for tea?' (On a gramophone record, half a century later, Peter Sellers played the chippy waitress who answered, 'Honey's off, dear.') By now the poem sounds intolerably affected. His poems of privilege seem now to reek of social superiority, like his clothes and hair-style. Those floppy locks!

The Brookean ideal persisted for a long time after his death, notably in those British movies that featured a gorgeous public schoolboy draping himself languidly over the inherited furni-ture. Even before I left Australia, I had noticed there was a distinct difference between Albert Finney and James Fox: Finney, though equipped with a charming smile, was no more exquisite than a turnip, whereas Fox was clearly the product of centuries of breeding. In fact he could have copied his floppy cowlick directly from photographs of Rupert Brooke, who was a film star *avant la lettre*.

But if the Grantchester poem, once famous, now looks like a fizzer, 'The Soldier', once thought jingoistic, now looks prescient in its consolatory lyricism. He wrote it as the massacre was beginning, and the subsequent slaughter confirmed the validity of his artistic impulse. In this poem, Brooke takes centre-screen as naturally as, not many years later, Laurence Olivier would do, when he played his Henry V as a Rupert Brooke-type: physically beautiful, smoothly eloquent, and able to vault without effort into the saddle of his waiting horse after delivering a long speech about the glories of England. 'In hearts at peace, under an English heaven.'

Though the line doesn't claim the whole of heaven for England, it makes clear that an English heaven is a privileged area. Members of the industrial proletariat might have felt otherwise, but they were not yet the typical voice of England: there was still a huge rural population who might not have felt that Brooke was being idealistic at all, but merely descriptive. He was a tremendous poetic talent, and those of his contemporaries who swooned over his potential were well justified. As the poem demonstrates, he had a way of putting the words together that combined the sonorities of the hymn book with the fluencies of contemporary speech. It was a rare knack, and became rarer still when his admirers, still dazzled by the glittering fluency of his verses, finally accepted the brutal fact that he would not be coming home.

Wedded

ISAAC ROSENBERG
(DURING THE FIRST WORLD WAR)

They leave their love-lorn haunts,
Their sigh-warm floating Eden;
And they are mute at once,
Mortals by God unheeden,
By their past kisses chidden.

But they have kist and known
Clear things we dim by guesses –
Spirit to spirit grown:
Heaven, born in hand-caresses.
Love, fall from sheltering tresses.

And they are dumb and strange:
Bared trees bowed from each other.
Their last green interchange
What lost dreams shall discover?
Dead, strayed, to love-strange lover.

WE MIGHT HAVE TO LOOK UP THE WORD 'CHIDDEN', BUT
otherwise this great poem is as clear as a teardrop. When we
think of the British poets lost in the First World War, we tend
to think principally of Wilfred Owen, and his priority in our

minds was justly earned. But we should also think of Isaac Rosenberg. Why don't we think of him straightaway? Partly, perhaps, because he was Jewish, and therefore doesn't strike us as a British poet in the first instance, but as some kind of exotic, foreign one. In fact he was no more foreign than London's East End, and he was greatly talented. Every Rosenberg poem is worth close study, but this one is the poem that got into my head all by itself, and has stayed there ever since, even as I am bent over from bowing out.

There is something wonderfully stately about its movement. The phrase 'their last green interchange' goes on burning, and the way the ordinary syntax is rearranged in the next part of the question is unforgettable even though it is clearly meant to be – a rare instance of a deliberate quirk attaining its aim. The drum beat of the last line, 'Dead, strayed, to love-strange lover', sounds like the slow march of a funeral, and a funeral, of course, is what this great poem was: the funeral of a generation.

Among its ghostly ranks, Rosenberg demands the same degree of attention as Owen, and perhaps he was even more musical. (Rosenberg seldom resorted to half-rhymes the way that Owen did and it's permissible to suggest that perhaps Rosenberg didn't need to. He simply found the musical range of pure rhyme sufficient.) There is no competition between the two young deaths, although one could still wish, even at this distance, that they had lived to compete in a different, peaceful world.

Another striking attribute of Rosenberg is that he could be funny about his own situation. There is a vivid passage in his fine poem 'Break of Day in the Trenches': 'Droll rat, they would shoot you if they knew / Your cosmopolitan sympathies . . .' The same poem has a famous image of the beautiful trench poppy, but it's the trench rat that is likely to capture our attention now, perhaps because 'cosmopolitan' was a term of denigration about Jews. In the long gaze of history, Rosenberg seems almost supernaturally aware of conflicts to come, but the immediate truth was that he had more than enough on his hands in the First World War, which cut him off from the poetic future that he would surely have adorned.

Not for That City

CHARLOTTE MEW
C. 1916

Not for that city of the level sun,
   Its golden streets and glittering gates ablaze –
   The shadeless, sleepless city of white days,
White nights, or nights and days that are as one –
We weary, when all is said, all thought, all done.
   We strain our eyes beyond this dusk to see
   What, from the threshold of eternity
We shall step into. No, I think we shun
The splendour of that everlasting glare,
   The clamour of that never-ending song.
   And if for anything we greatly long,
It is for some remote and quiet stair
   Which winds to silence and a space for sleep
   Too sound for waking and for dreams too deep.

SOME OF CHARLOTTE MEW'S BEST POEMS ARE TRICKY TO
reprint because she often wrote in long lines. She could afford
to do this because she had a faultless sense of rhythm. The only
rhythmic glitch in this poem is when she forgets that it has been
a long time since the reader saw the first line, so she starts the
fifth line ('We weary . . .') without the necessary acknowledge-
ment of what we are wearying of. But we can reach a sufficient

appreciation of her stately prosodic luxuriance simply by reciting 'The splendour of that everlasting glare, / The clamour of that never-ending song.'

The metrical progress of her sense of form had the impressive weight of a slowly moving train, but it was a train that was clearly going somewhere, through relished landscapes, searching for stillness and quiet after a long struggle. Born into a family racked by childhood death, insolvency and mental illness, she compensated for the instability by sticking, metrically, to a measured poetic tranquillity that some today might call severe.

Charlotte Mew should be much better known than she is. She had some significant literary champions in her own time, but financial and family troubles continued to dog her, and she was eventually committed to an institution, where she killed herself. A biography like that might enhance the stature of a male poet but she dates from an era when a woman who dressed like W.B. Yeats was unlikely to be given credit for her bardic aspirations, even by W.B. Yeats. (My mental picture of Charlotte Mew is always mixed up with the hushed and mysterious appearances of Miss Froy, the British woman spy in the well-cut tweeds who enlists the aid of Michael Redgrave and Margaret Lockwood in *The Lady Vanishes*.)

Yasmin (A Ghazel)

James Elroy Flecker

c. 1916

How splendid in the morning grows the lily: with what grace
 he throws
His supplication to the rose: do roses nod the head, Yasmin?

But when the silver dove descends I find the little flower of friends
Whose very name that sweetly ends I say when I have said,
 Yasmin.

The morning light is clear and cold: I dare not in that light behold
A whiter light, a deeper gold, a glory too far shed, Yasmin.

But when the deep red light of day is level with the lone highway,
And some to Meccah turn to pray, and I toward thy bed, Yasmin;

Or when the wind beneath the moon is drifting like a soul aswoon,
And harping planets talk love's tune with milky wings
 outspread, Yasmin,

Shower down thy love, O burning bright! For one night or the
 other night,
Will come the Gardener in white, and gathered flowers are
 dead, Yasmin.

THE DEFINITION OF *GHAZEL* – AN ARABIC LYRIC POEM that begins with a rhymed couplet whose rhyme is repeated in all even lines and that is especially common in Persian literature – is enough to put us into the old, tourist vision of the unfamiliar and voluptuous lands that supposedly lay East of Suez. This poem by James Elroy Flecker was a big hit at the time, back there before the Great War had finished changing the world: and it's still got its *misterioso* fascination. Like a quivering, powdered cube of Turkish delight, it gives us a delicious if slightly synthetic taste of the exotic east. Its belly-dancing rhythms are in the same tent, as it were, as the quatrains of the *Rubaiyat* of Omar Khayyam, as translated by Edward Fitzgerald. Flecker was so sinuously rhythmic you could dance to him.

Like the *Rubaiyat*, but with a concentration of effect all its own, 'Yasmin' revels in its own effects of finger-cymbals and nose flutes. 'Or when the wind beneath the moon is drifting like a soul aswoon, / And harping planets talk love's tune with milky wings outspread, Yasmin'. Recovering temporarily from his intoxication, the swooning reader might ask why the planets are harping, or perhaps what they are harping on, but Flecker's gift for impetus works deftly to sideline any niggling questions. The whole thing goes forward like a caravan of camels, but if startled, the reader feels, they could gallop like racing dromedaries.

Golden journeys were Flecker's speciality. *The Golden Journey to Samarkand*, when equipped with music by Delius, appeared in theatres under the title *Hassan*. The BBC once did a fabulous black-and-white dramatisation of *Hassan* starring Sir John Gielgud, with the beautiful Nyree Dawn Porter as the fascinating female incarnation of the Arabic East. The modern age of the permanent television memory had not yet arrived, so the show is gone now. I can remember that despite the absurd lushness of its language, it held the screen as a drama.

Flecker's equating of Yasmin's bed with Mecca would have put him in danger in a later day, but in those days the East was still an Imperial possession, in the sense that you could write poetry about its supposed wonders without running any risks of opprobrium or revenge. In other words, Flecker's poetic creations about the magnetically exotic East are acts of imperialism. But so, in a way, is almost all of literature, from Homer onwards: the annexations never stop.

Anthem for Doomed Youth

WILFRED OWEN

1917

What passing-bells for these who die as cattle?
　　Only the monstrous anger of the guns.
　　Only the stuttering rifles' rapid rattle
Can patter out their hasty orisons.
No mockeries now for them; no prayers nor bells;
　　Nor any voice of mourning save the choirs, –
The shrill, demented choirs of wailing shells;
　　And bugles calling for them from sad shires.

What candles may be held to speed them all?
　　Not in the hands of boys, but in their eyes
Shall shine the holy glimmers of goodbyes.
　　The pallor of girls' brows shall be their pall;
Their flowers the tenderness of patient minds,
And each slow dusk a drawing-down of blinds.

———

WHEN W.B. YEATS DID HIS 1935 REVISION OF *THE OXFORD Book of Modern Verse* he left Owen and the other war poets out. It is necessary to remember this fact when assessing just how bright Yeats was. Sometimes he could be a fool, and he was certainly a fool when he gave the elbow to Owen, who emerged from the war as probably the greatest poet to have taken part in it.

But if you couldn't get Owen's poem from the Oxford book, you could get it from *The Albatross Book of Living Verse*, which was one of my first-year text-books at Sydney University in the late 1950s. Owen's poem knocked me sideways, and especially with the finale. 'The pallor of girls' brows' is a pretty generous image from someone who was probably more interested in the pallid brows of boys. But really this poem gets you beyond gender, as indeed death does. Perhaps he was thinking of that: he had been lucky so far, but not long afterwards the luck ran out. 'And each slow dusk a drawing-down of blinds.' I have thought about that a lot lately, rather tending, in this slow dusk, to ask for the blinds not to be drawn, but to be lifted.

It was Owen's reputation that emerged from the war, I should have said. He himself was killed in the last week. When I first got to London in the early sixties, Benjamin Britten's *War Requiem* was being launched at the Albert Hall, and I must say that his setting of Owen's poem seemed to me hopelessly trivial. But I soon learned not to be too forthcoming with this opinion. Even at this distance, the United Kingdom's experience of the First World War is still not something to be frivolous about: the memory burned deep and lasting, like phosphorus under water.

La Figlia Che Piange

T. S. ELIOT

1917

O quam te memorem virgo

Stand on the highest pavement of the stair –
Lean on a garden urn –
Weave, weave the sunlight in your hair –
Clasp your flowers to you with a pained surprise –
Fling them to the ground and turn
With a fugitive resentment in your eyes:
But weave, weave the sunlight in your hair.

So I would have had him leave,
So I would have had her stand and grieve,
So he would have left
As the soul leaves the body torn and bruised,
As the mind deserts the body it has used.
I should find
Some way incomparably light and deft,
Some way we both should understand,
Simple and faithless as a smile and shake of the hand.

She turned away, but with the autumn weather
Compelled my imagination many days,
Many days and many hours:
Her hair over her arms and her arms full of flowers.
And I wonder how they should have been together!

I should have lost a gesture and a pose.
Sometimes these cogitations still amaze
The troubled midnight and the noon's repose.

EVERYONE AT SYDNEY UNIVERSITY WITH LITERARY
pretensions in the late 1950s was still busy being bowled over
by T.S. Eliot's *The Waste Land* when his *Four Quartets*, after the
long trip from England, snuck up on them and knocked them
flat. My friend Robert Hughes – gone now, alas – could recite
the whole of *Four Quartets* from memory. I couldn't quite do
that, but I could carry on with the next bit after hearing any line
in it, and I knew quite a few of Eliot's shorter poems by heart,
including this one. 'Weave, weave the sunlight in your hair'. I
probably looked silly saying it, but its rhythms were infectiously
percussive. Reportedly, Eliot was astonished by how often he
was asked to recite it.

The poem is a showcase for his repertoire of technical tricks.
He could put a verse paragraph seductively off the beat, as it
were, as in:

Some way incomparably light and deft
Some way we both should understand

Two lines of deliberate vagueness led up to a clinching line of
killing specificity:

Simple and faithless as a smile and shake of the hand.

One didn't ask, at the time, why the smile had to be faithless. One just lay back and got carried away in the rush, like the male ballet dancer doing nothing except making one *jetée* entrance after another, or flinging himself to the floor in order to look upwards at his pointed toe.

There was quite a lot of flash furniture to get past before the reciter started turning tip-toe pirouettes. The title, I learned, was in Italian, and meant 'The Girl Who Cries'. The epigraph was from the *Aeneid*, whatever that was: 'How should I remember you, maiden?' I was still a barbarian at the time, and never suspected that Virgil would, one day soon, overwhelm me and carry me off through the empty halls of Dis into the inane regions. *Perque domos Ditis vacuas et inania regna.*

An Irish Airman Foresees His Death

W.B. YEATS
1919

I know that I shall meet my fate
Somewhere among the clouds above;
Those that I fight I do not hate
Those that I guard I do not love;
My country is Kiltartan Cross,
My countrymen Kiltartan's poor,
No likely end could bring them loss
Or leave them happier than before.
Nor law, nor duty bade me fight,
Nor public man, nor cheering crowds,
A lonely impulse of delight
Drove to this tumult in the clouds;
I balanced all, brought all to mind,
The years to come seemed waste of breath,
A waste of breath the years behind
In balance with this life, this death.

———

THIS WHOLE POEM IS AS CLEAR CUT AS A JOUST: THAT,
indeed, is its context, medieval gallantry with pretty wings and
reciprocating engines. Yeats saw the romance of the business,
without even having to go to the war. Daringly, the poem's range
of tones includes the possibility that fighting for your life might

be quite exciting: indeed the height of the romantic action. That being said, it is possible to ask if Yeats had really understood what was at stake.

Yeats famously left the British war poets out of his 1936 edition of *The Oxford Book of Modern Verse*. He seems to have thought that the Great War was no fit subject for poetry. A strange idea on his part, perhaps, but he could have backed it up by saying, truly, that he himself wrote little about it at the time, being more preoccupied with trouble at home. As the war on the Continent developed into a mass mutual slaughter, it was remarkable how he, as a poet, declined to notice.

It could be said that he had other things on his plate: as an Irishman he was bound to see the war in the streets as a tumult more immediate than anything happening overseas. Well before 1919, when he published the poem, the romantic death of a single airman had ceased to be a very illustrative subject – whole regiments of soldiers had been buried in the earth without having seen even a moment's glory – but Yeats moved on, in his post-war writings, in ways that opened up a greater emotional scope, even though he never quite came to the point of dealing with the brute earthly facts of an epochal conflict.

'Sailing to Byzantium', the masterpiece that starts 'That is no country for old men', is one of the star poems in his collection *The Tower*, a book so crammed with wonderful things that it could have served him as the summary of his whole poetic career. A transition is marked by these two poems ('An Irish Airman Foresees His Death' and 'Sailing to Byzantium') from the traditional to the modern, from poems whose meaning you can't mistake to poems whose meaning you can never quite be sure of. If such parallels were helpful, one could say that something like the quantum theory, or something even more like the uncertainty principle, had arrived in the field of literature.

'Sailing to Byzantium' heads towards mysticism, but only the phrase 'perne in a gyre' is a mystery. In my view it should be left that way. Though whole theses have been devoted to Yeats's mystical concepts, he is, in fact, at his weakest when he only half knows what he means. ('Perne' is a word he made up, and it is remarkable how it has failed to catch on, even after decades of explanatory scholarship.)

Only a few lines away we will find a phrase as concretely evocative as 'mackerel-crowded seas'. When one visualises the mackerel bumping into each other it makes any amount of gyre-perning seem very abstract. A good moment to remember that Yeats was a truly great poet, with a wealth of vocabulary that really needed no additional mystical accoutrements, and indeed from his later poetry they were largely banished. His later poetry is consistently magnificent, so it was a surprise when Professor Ricks called it mere rhetoric. The professor deserves credit for his adventurousness as a critic, but if Yeats's later poetry is mere rhetoric then I am a Dutchman with wooden clogs.

'Among School Children' is the later Yeats at his very greatest. The children watch him walk slowly past as if he were indeed what he was, a living monument. Unfortunately, in real life, he had forgotten his dignity almost entirely and was treating himself with monkey-gland injections, thus to restore his virility, which he expended on a platoon of progressively younger women.

His patient wife, George, spoke only the truth when she said that his opinions about life were trivial unless they were expressed in the form of poetry. But it remains unarguable that most of the poetry is hard to forget, even the early poems when they are still wreathed in the faery mists through which a frail boat comes gliding across the water, bearing some ethereal princess to her destiny. And some of the later poems are beyond criticism, even beyond admiration. One could wish that he had not brought back the gyres in the wonderful 'Under Ben Bulben', but one is not likely to forget that poem's last exhortation:

> Cast a cold eye
> On life, on death.
>> Horseman, pass by!

I'm practising my cold eye now, and doing my best not to think of those monkey-gland injections.

Wild Peaches

ELINOR WYLIE
1920

1

When the world turns completely upside down
You say we'll emigrate to the Eastern Shore
Aboard a river-boat from Baltimore;
We'll live among wild peach trees, miles from town,
You'll wear a coonskin cap, and I a gown
Homespun, dyed butternut's dark gold color.
Lost, like your lotus-eating ancestor,
We'll swim in milk and honey till we drown.

The winter will be short, the summer long,
The autumn amber-hued, sunny and hot,
Tasting of cider and of scuppernong;
All seasons sweet, but autumn best of all.
The squirrels in their silver fur will fall
Like falling leaves, like fruit, before your shot.

2

The autumn frosts will lie upon the grass
Like bloom on grapes of purple-brown and gold.
The misted early mornings will be cold;
The little puddles will be roofed with glass.

The sun, which burns from copper into brass,
Melts these at noon, and makes the boys unfold
Their knitted mufflers; full as they can hold,
Fat pockets dribble chestnuts as they pass.

Peaches grow wild, and pigs can live in clover;
A barrel of salted herrings lasts a year;
The spring begins before the winter's over.
By February you may find the skins
Of garter snakes and water moccasins
Dwindled and harsh, dead-white and cloudy-clear.

3

When April pours the colors of a shell
Upon the hills, when every little creek
Is shot with silver from the Chesapeake
In shoals new-minted by the ocean swell,
When strawberries go begging, and the sleek
Blue plums lie open to the blackbird's beak,
We shall live well—we shall live very well.

The months between the cherries and the peaches
Are brimming cornucopias which spill
Fruits red and purple, somber-bloomed and black;
Then, down rich fields and frosty river beaches
We'll trample bright persimmons, while you kill
Bronze partridge, speckled quail, and canvas-back.

Down to the Puritan marrow of my bones
There's something in this richness that I hate.
I love the look, austere, immaculate,
Of landscapes drawn in pearly monotones.
There's something in my very blood that owns
Bare hills, cold silver on a sky of slate,
A thread of water, churned to milky spate
Streaming through slanted pastures fenced with stones.

I love those skies, thin blue or snowy gray,
Those fields sparse-planted, rendering meager sheaves;
That spring, briefer than apple-blossom's breath,
Summer, so much too beautiful to stay,
Swift autumn, like a bonfire of leaves,
And sleepy winter, like the sleep of death.

————

AS THIS GREAT POEM REVEALS, ELINOR WYLIE'S TECHNIQUE
was perfection. Even a skint poet dedicated to the forthcoming
proletarian revolution might have thought about the first stanza:
'God! I wish I'd written that. What control of pace it's got. The
music, the vocabulary: it's all there.' Even the weird word 'scup-
pernong' proves to be a perfect fit, after you've looked it up.

Between the wars, Elinor Wylie was the complete American
aristocratic blue-stocking: stately of aspect, high-born, bril-
liantly married, artistically talented and totally loaded. The
reader might like to compare this poem with an apparently

similar creation by her British equivalent, Vita Sackville-West, who had all those qualities too, except the last: Vita's gardens at Sissinghurst were really the only thing she owned. Elinor Wylie owned everything, including all the land as far as her eyes could see. But she manages to give the impression, in this poem, that she arrived in America on the *Mayflower* only a few days before, and built, bare-handed, a log cabin with an outside loo.

For most of the poem you would swear that her love of the land – so detailed, so penetrating, so evocative – was at the core of her simple soul. Unexpectedly, however, she switches tone in the last section, and claims that she is alienated from all the natural lushness she has been evoking. Look closely at the start of the stanza in which she shifts the tone, and indeed the subject. The change of gear is deliberately brutal: of the kind that leaves your transmission full of steel filings.

It turns out that she does not love the plentiful life at all, where the forest is a playground in a push-button panorama. Oh no: she is an austere person. You would scarcely think that her financial resources were infinite. The implausibility, however, is negated by the consideration that her poem reflects two states of soul that really can exist within the same person: the love of luxury and the thirst for austerity. Just as Marie Antoinette built the Petit Trianon so that she could wear a dirndl and skip around worrying her sheep, millionaires really do sometimes build huts for themselves, and this virtuoso piece was the equivalent of that: she is grasping at authenticity.

Her most famous novel, *The Venetian Glass Nephew*, is read now only by PhD students, poor doomed creatures. Poised and pirouetting for each conceit, poetic in the most brittle way, it tells a story as artificial as its title; and there were other books that verged on the preciously glossy; and far too many poems that did the same. Like so much decor of the period, the typical Wylie poem has gone a paler pastel with time, like an art nouveau luxury powder compact left too long in the light. But what matters is what she was capable of when she rebelled against herself, and this great poem is a fine example of what can be achieved when you go in for a bare-knuckle fight against your own soul. She was a luxury girl, and here she is in the woods, fighting wolves bare-handed. She died young, from a stroke, and one feels the loss even now.

The Emperor of Ice-Cream

WALLACE STEVENS

1922

Call the roller of big cigars,
The muscular one, and bid him whip
In kitchen cups concupiscent curds.
Let the wenches dawdle in such dress
As they are used to wear, and let the boys
Bring flowers in last month's newspapers.
Let be be finale of seem.
The only emperor is the emperor of ice-cream.

Take from the dresser of deal,
Lacking the three glass knobs, that sheet
On which she embroidered fantails once
And spread it so as to cover her face.
If her horny feet protrude, they come
To show how cold she is, and dumb.
Let the lamp affix its beam.
The only emperor is the emperor of ice-cream.

———

THIS IS WALLACE STEVENS IN HIS EARLY MOOD, THE
mood that I like best. Later on, he got overblown in his own
manner – the most perilous state a poet can get into. But early
on, his images were separately intelligible and vivid, without

getting lost in the deadly blend of fluency. Though his bourgeois dependability might have been the secret of his relentless output, in the long run it was bad for him to be an insurance broker. He might have been better off fighting sharks.

I learned this most famous of his early poems by heart, and thought that there might be other poems later on which might prove equally attractive; but although they tried, they were not. The phrase 'delicious fantasy' applies to some of the work in *Harmonium*, but later on Stevens matured into a fluent fossil. In this poem the images are vital even when they are contestable as to their truth. The concupiscent curds in the kitchen cups still seem to me to be meaningless if strictly analysed, yet when taken in at the hurtling pace dictated by the rhythm they are deliciously full of meaning, particularly because the line is such fun to say. In fact, 'The Emperor of Ice-Cream' was such fun to say that I had to be physically restrained from saying it, and even today I have a tendency to rattle it off as a party piece. There is a must-speak quality to the whole poem. As so often happens, must-speak means must-remember.

Every image in 'The Emperor of Ice-Cream' is radiant if inexplicable. While I was writing this note it was pointed out to me that the whole poem is a prelude to a funeral. I had never noticed. The thought should have occurred to me, but I spent a lifetime being too carried away by the vivid rhythm of the images. Unfortunately, however, too many of Stevens' later poems, especially the larger ones, were glued together by portentousness. He overworked the trick of lining up the meanings of a word and choosing the meaning a few places away from the one that first occurred to him: a sure-fire formula for a writer to produce semi-surrealist mush.

In a famous poem like 'Sunday Morning' there is deliberate

finessing going on, to hide the sense. There are some who think that the end of 'Sunday Morning' is unbeatable but I insist on pointing out that the ending is overloaded with portent and has Significant Ending written all over it. The bird that goes downward to darkness 'on extended wings' had certainly better have its wings extended, or it would plummet vertically and land on its head. Or, more likely, it would never take off, as so many poems by the supposedly mature Stevens didn't.

The famous lunch date on Key West featuring Stevens and Robert Frost remains one of my favourite trade-talk stories. When they agreed that they preferred 'separable' poems, they were agreeing that they liked their own stuff.

One Perfect Rose

DOROTHY PARKER
1923

A single flow'r he sent me, since we met.
　　All tenderly his messenger he chose;
Deep-hearted, pure, with scented dew still wet—
　　One perfect rose.

I knew the language of the floweret;
　　'My fragile leaves,' it said, 'his heart enclose.'
Love long has taken for his amulet
　　One perfect rose.

Why is it no one ever sent me yet
　　One perfect limousine, do you suppose?
Ah no, it's always just my luck to get
　　One perfect rose.

——————

AS A DRAMA CRITIC ('*THE HOUSE BEAUTIFUL* IS THE PLAY lousy') Dorothy Parker was better than as a film critic, and even as a film critic she was a lot better than average, but finally she was lazy, and usually she was lazy because she had recently been drunk, and was gathering her strength to get that way again.

But a poem of this quality is enough on its own to prove that she took by right her place at the Algonquin Round Table of convivial wits. Some of the attendees rehearsed their spontaneity beforehand and she might have done the same, but her poems stay good. (One of her short stories is in the same glittering class: don't miss 'The Waltz', which shows a complete mastery of the interior monologue as a form, and which is still funny and touching eighty years later.) Trained in the economies that make the act of writing more bearable for anyone who would rather be lying down instead, she had the gifts required to put a lot of thought and emotion into a short space. 'Deep-hearted, pure, with scented dew still wet' gives you all you need to see of the rose without grappling with the cellophane that wraps it up.

She hated the solitude that any writer had better learn to love, or else a killing vice often awaits. Legend has it (it has too damned much about her) that she guaranteed a steady supply of short-stay male visitors to the office where she sat solitary: she ordered that the word MEN be painted on her door. Such charming stories do something to offset the haunting picture of her final chaos. They also embody the deep rhythm of her talent: long thought, and then the sudden thrust of the stiletto.

Unlike Ogden Nash and Don Marquis, Parker made a point of writing the kind of poems-for-periodicals that were actually poetry, and not non-poetry. (Nash could pull off the occasional mini-masterpiece such as 'parsley / is gharsley', and Marquis's *Archy and Mehitabel* poems added up to a reliable vaudeville routine, but on the whole we do best to avoid the American habit of saluting anything billed as Humor and abasing ourselves before the fecundity of its creators.) A better place to search for inventive word play is among the comic strips. (In Walt Kelly's *Pogo* strip there was an explosive personal appearance by Strawberry Shortcake, the Baton Rouge Bombshell. I'm still laughing.) Parker, on her small scale, could be truly witty, and you simply can't buy a reliable lifetime supply of wit. Sometimes you have to wait. Wit, wait: the words are close.

Captain Carpenter

JOHN CROWE RANSOM
1924

Captain Carpenter rose up in his prime
   Put on his pistols and went riding out
But had got well-nigh nowhere at that time
   Till he fell in with ladies in a rout.

It was a pretty lady and all her train
   That played with him so sweetly but before
An hour she'd taken a sword with all her main
   And twined him of his nose for evermore.

Captain Carpenter mounted another day
   And straightway rode into a surly rogue
That looked unchristian but be that as may
   The captain did not wait upon prologue.

But drew upon him out of his great heart
   The other swung against him with a club
And cracked his two legs at the shinny part
   And let him roll and stick like any tub.

Captain Carpenter rode many a time
   From male and female took he sundry harms
And met the wife of Satan crying 'I'm
   The she-wolf bids you shall bear no more arms.'

Their strokes and counters whistled in the wind
    I would he had delivered half his blows
But where she should have made off like a hind
    The bitch bit off his arms at the elbows.

Captain Carpenter parted with his ears
    To a surly rogue that used him in this wise
O Jesus ere his threescore and ten years
    Another had pinched out his sweet blue eyes.

Captain Carpenter got up on his roan
    And sallied from the gate for hell's despite
I heard him asking in the grimmest tone
    If any enemies yet there were to fight?

'Is there an adversary drunk with fame
    Who will risk to be wounded by my tongue
Or burnt in two beneath my red heart's flame
    These are the perils he is cast among.

'But if he can he has a pretty choice
    From an anatomy with little to lose
Whether he cut my tongue and take my voice
    Or whether it be my round red heart he choose.'

It was the neatest knave that ever was seen
    Stepping in perfume from his lady's bower
Who on this word put in his merry mien
    And fell on Captain Carpenter like a tower.

I would not knock old fellows in the dust
    But there lay Captain Carpenter on his back
His weapons were the stout heart in his bust
    And a blade shook between rotten teeth alack.

The rogue in scarlet and grey soon knew his mind
    He wished to get his trophy and depart
With gentle apology and touch refined
    He pierced him and produced the captain's heart.

God's mercy rest on Captain Carpenter now
    I thought him sirs an honest gentleman
Citizen husband soldier and scholar enow
    Let jangling kites eat of him if they can.

But God's deep curses follow after those
    That shore him of his goodly nose and ears
His legs and strong arms at the two elbows
    And eyes that had not watered seventy years.

The curse of hell upon the sleek upstart
    That got the captain finally on his back
And took the red red vitals of his heart
    And made the kites to whet their beaks clack clack.

———

I FORGET HOW JOHN CROWE RANSOM'S GREATLY WEIRD
yet weirdly great poem about Captain Carpenter reached us in
Australia. In my mind it arrived welded to the bottom of a ship,

like a consignment of radioactive diamonds. All I recall is that it shook us all up through being so unlike anything we had ever seen come out of America. Was it about the Civil War? And if so, which side was Captain Carpenter on?

He was on both sides, and the war was from any time that still had swords, even if pistols were also in the picture. As the protagonist is serially reduced to his component parts, the poet is mounting a whirlwind attack on ordinary expectation. Lines keep heading off in directions you don't expect them to, and even the most solid rhyme can have an air of approximation, as if it were there only for temporary use, like the human body. We can see how 'surly rogue' might call up 'prologue' but it sounds like a shaky phonetic connection. More disturbingly still, it seems proud to be: the whole poem flaunts a bubbling confidence in the defiance of rules. The poet knows what the rules are, but he prefers kicking them to pieces.

Finally defiance is what the poem embodies. As the Captain's body is reduced to a stub, there is an argument building up: the rebellious contention that all expectations are back to being at hazard. High time, then, to look Ransom up, where we find him firmly contextualised in the old South: until quite late in his life he was a leading light of the Southern Agrarians (it was a literary movement, not a farmers' association) who frowned on the advance of industrial civilisation. A lot of the energy in his poems went into turning back the clock. The clock, however, tends to resist.

Craftsmen

VITA SACKVILLE-WEST
1926

All craftsmen share a knowledge. They have held
Reality down fluttering to a bench;
Cut wood to their own purposes; compelled
The growth of pattern with the patient shuttle;
Drained acres to a trench.

  Control is theirs. They have ignored the subtle
Release of spirit from the jail of shape.

  They have been concerned with prison, not escape;
Pinioned the fact, and let the rest go free,
And out of need made inadvertent art.
All things designed to play a faithful part
Build up their plain particular poetry.

  Tools have their own integrity;
The sneath of scythe curves rightly to the hand,
The hammer knows its balance, knife its edge.
All tools inevitably planned,
Stout friends, with pledge
Of service; with their crotchets too
That masters understand,
And proper character, and separate heart,
But always to their chosen temper true.
 – So language, smithied at the common fire,
Grew to its use; as sneath and shank and haft
Of well-grained wood, nice instruments of craft,
Curve to the simple mould the hands require,

Born of the needs of man.
The poet like the artisan
Works lonely with his tools; picks up each one,
Blunt mallet knowing, and the quick thin blade,
And plane that travels when the hewing's done;
Rejects, and chooses; scores a fresh faint line;
Sharpens, intent upon his chiselling;
Bends lower to examine his design,
If it be truly made,
And brings perfection to so slight a thing
But in the shadows of his working-place,
Dust-moted, dim,
Among the chips and lumber of his trade,
Lifts never his bowed head, a breathing-space
To look upon the world beyond the sill,
The world framed small, in distance, for to him
   The world and all its weight are in his will.
   Yet in the ecstasy of his rapt mood
   There's no retreat his spirit cannot fill,
   No distant leagues, no present, and no past,
No essence that his need may not distil,
All pressed into his service, but he knows
   Only the immediate care, if that be good;
The little focus that his words enclose;
As the poor joiner, working at his wood,
Knew not the tree from which the planks were taken,
Knew not the glade from which the trunk was brought,
Knew not the soil in which the roots were fast,
Nor by what centuries of gales the boughs were shaken,
But holds them all beneath his hands at last.

———

Fans of Virginia Woolf's bisexual novel *Orlando* will know that its gender-fluid hero/heroine was based on Vita Sackville-West. But we should remind ourselves that in real life Vita made a pretty good show of domestic stability. Her husband Harold Nicolson was also same-sex oriented, so it balanced out. Meanwhile Vita spent a lot of time in the garden, and she was also a handy carpenter, as this poem proves. When Philip Larkin assembled his *Oxford Book of Twentieth Century English Verse*, he included this poem, and it was a particular focal point of hatred for those younger than he who had been left out of the anthology. They had dedicated their lives to poetry and here was a musty old Georgian fossil like Vita being dug up again.

In fact the author of a poem as good as this can never die. Compulsory quotability is a form of immortality, and this stretch of verse, from the start to where Larkin chose to finish it (there was more) is stunningly accomplished in every line and turn of line, quite apart from the fact that its observations were so concrete and precise. On the strength of this, there was nothing she couldn't write in verse; there was only the mystery of why she chose not to do more poems like it. Perhaps she was too busy chasing Violet Trefusis. When they caught up with each other they both became even more busy, and looking back one has to grasp that the literary achievements of any of them, Harold included, had to be fitted into a pretty complicated emotional traffic jam.

But back to the poem, which is still driving forward without us. Anyone who has done any carpentry, or even just done a few lessons of it in school, will know that fluttering is just the right word for what a long strip of wood does if it is held down to be worked on at the bench. Similarly evocative accuracies keep on cropping up, as the poem twists and turns on its way forward, like a porpoise riding the bow-wave of a ship. She was very smooth, for someone with so much to say, or anyway, she had a lot to say that day. There is a lot of other poetry by her, and most of it is very dull. All the more amazing, then, that when she suddenly decided to, she could be as brilliant as this. After we have looked up the word 'sneath', we realise that in fact this is a poetic excursus remarkably short of obscure words. Her metrically short lines are brilliantly placed. The young post-war poets who resented seeing her name included in Larkin's anthology should have asked themselves whether really, honestly and truly, they thought that they were as accomplished as she. On the whole, they weren't. Larkin wasn't going to reject an achievement like this for some little poem that he felt had cost the poet nothing. This is great work.

On the level of verbal carpentry, Vita's control of the narrative flow depends largely on how she can break into the iambic pentameter verse paragraph without hobbling the pace. The occasional tetrameter or trimeter clicks into position with barely a shudder. Would-be poets who are foolish enough to think that this trick might be easy should be warned that it is wise to get plenty of practice making the pentameters match exactly before you break into them with a shorter line. The deadly interaction of a pentameter that doesn't scan properly and a short line that doesn't scan properly either has reduced many a recent poem to a shambling wreck, apparently without the poet in question even noticing that the car has crashed across the traffic island and crumpled its nose against a concrete bollard. It's the illusion of heady progress that brings on the madness: on the page of one's composition book, a poem isn't necessarily sustaining its impetus just because it seems to move forward. It might be headed towards oblivion.

Choosing a Mast

ROY CAMPBELL
1931

This mast, new-shaved, through whom I rive the ropes,
Says she was once an oread of the slopes,
Graceful and tall upon the rocky highlands,
A slender tree, as vertical as noon,
And her low voice was lovely as the silence
Through which a fountain whistles to the moon,
Who now of the white spray must take the veil
And, for her songs, the thunder of the sail.

I chose her for her fragrance, when the spring
With sweetest resins swelled her fourteenth ring
And with live amber welded her young thews:
I chose her for the glory of the Muse,
Smoother of forms, that her hard-knotted grain,
Grazed by the chisel, shaven by the plane,
Might from the steel as cool a burnish take
As from the bladed moon a windless lake.

I chose her for her eagerness of flight
Where she stood tiptoe on the rocky height
Lifted by her own perfume to the sun,
While through her rustling plumes with eager sound
Her eagle spirit, with the gale at one,
Spreading wide pinions, would have spurned the ground

And her own sleeping shadow, had they not
With thymy fragrance charmed her to the spot.

Lover of song, I chose this mountain pine
Not only for the straightness of her spine
But for her songs: for there she loved to sing
Through a long noon's repose of wave and wing –
The fluvial swirling of her scented hair
Sole rill of song in all that windless air
And her slim form the naiad of the stream
Afloat upon the languor of its theme;

And for the soldier's fare on which she fed –
Her wine the azure, and the snow her bread;
And for her stormy watches on the height –
For only out of solitude or strife
Are born the sons of valour and delight;
And lastly for her rich exulting life
That with the wind stopped not its singing breath
But carolled on, the louder for its death.

Under a pine, when summer days were deep,
We loved the most to lie in love or sleep:
And when in long hexameters the west
Rolled his grey surge, the forest for his lyre,
It was the pines that sang us to our rest
Loud in the wind and fragrant in the fire,
With legioned voices swelling all night long,
From Pelion to Provence, their storm of song.

It was the pines that fanned us in the heat,
The pines, that cheered us in the time of sleet,
For which sweet gifts I set one dryad free –
No longer to the wind a rooted foe,
This nymph shall wander where she longs to be
And with the blue north wind arise and go,
A silver huntress with the moon to run
And fly through rainbows with the rising sun;

And when to pasture in the glittering shoals
The guardian mistral drives his thundering foals,
And when like Tartar horsemen racing free
We ride the snorting fillies of the sea,
My pine shall be the archer of the gale
While on the bending willow curves the sail
From whose great bow the long keel shooting home
Shall fly, the feathered arrow of the foam.

———

POSSESSING THE DYNAMISM TO MAKE COUPLETS FLOW,
Roy Campbell could make the thump of his straining sail
match the beating of your heart. 'Choosing a Mast' is a bit long
for a short poem, but there is nothing loose about it: it goes
like a thoroughbred horse – always one of his favourite icons.
(His autobiography *Light on a Dark Horse* can be recom-
mended for its vivid self-obsession.) Campbell gets the danger
into the poem just by the way he can evoke the tautness of the
sail, filled by the rushing air. 'My pine shall be the archer of

the gale' gets the speed and tension of the straining mast into the prosody.

By the end of the poem he is talking about horses and boats as if they were the one thing, and indeed each in his mind was an ideal combination of strength and speed. You can imagine him bursting into a London editor's office, parking his riding boots on the desk, and getting into a punch-up with any frail Thirties poet who happened to wander in. With a bleak eye cast at MacNeice, Spender, Auden and Day-Lewis, he was the satirist who invented the compound poetic identity, MacSpaunday. His pose of individuality was not entirely unjustified. To one degree or another, all of MacSpaunday's components fell into the left-wing line. Campbell was out there on the right, fighting for Franco.

As well as a short epic like this one, he could write long epics too, but most of his long poems have dated fiercely, although his satire *The Georgiad* – a supposedly rollicking send-up of such milquetoast Georgian poets as Lascelles Abercrombie and John Drinkwater – remains a key area of research for any scholars who might still wonder if the Georgian movement reigned as a dominant hegemony. It didn't dominate Campbell, that's for sure.

Nothing did. Being dauntless was Campbell's shtick. How many poets have gone out in a boat alone and faced the roaring waves? It's not the same as catching the Channel ferry. We might also ask how many Thirties poets, at the time of the Spanish Civil War, not only put their money on Franco but joined his army. Campbell was the one. Although it might be thought that he put himself into an embarrassing position, in the long gaze of history it can't be denied that he was among the first literary figures who got it right about Stalin.

Soldier, scholar, horseman he (here I borrow the encomium that Yeats devised to fit his hard-riding hero Major Robert Gregory), Campbell was entirely without humility at a time when men with a similar deficiency were tearing the world to pieces, but his powers of creativity still look impressive even today, and it would be nice to think that his gift for the lyrical cadence saved him from the worst excesses of strutting around with his hand in the air. Campbell scarcely rates now as an attractive figure, but for any reader with an ear for his driving rhythms he is sure to remain a forceful poet.

somewhere i have never travelled

E.E. CUMMINGS

1931

somewhere i have never travelled, gladly beyond
any experience, your eyes have their silence:
in your most frail gesture are things which enclose me,
or which i cannot touch because they are too near

your slightest look easily will unclose me
though i have closed myself as fingers,
you open always petal by petal myself as Spring opens
(touching skilfully, mysteriously) her first rose

or if your wish be to close me, i and
my life will shut very beautifully, suddenly,
as when the heart of this flower imagines
the snow carefully everywhere descending;

nothing which we are to perceive in this world equals
the power of your intense fragility: whose texture
compels me with the colour of its countries,
rendering death and forever with each breathing

(i do not know what it is about you that closes
and opens; only something in me understands
the voice of your eyes is deeper than all roses)
nobody, not even the rain, has such small hands

BACK THERE IN THE LATE 1950S I WENT CRAZY ABOUT
several modern poets – about Ezra Pound I went almost as
crazy as he was – but the one who really got into my blood-
stream was E. E. Cummings (still spelling his name in lower
case in those days) to the extent that I tried to convince myself
he was a genius in all departments. Several of my fellow inhab-
itants of Sydney University's artistic netherworld shared the
same admiration and one of them, a budding theatrical pro-
ducer, staged a production of Cummings's play *him*, whose
insanely eccentric verbal pyrotechnics might have been designed
to send the audience screaming back into the street even before
the leading actor had to be sedated in his dressing room, his
blood-vessels bursting from the strain of remembering speeches
a block long.

A sure-fire flop anywhere in the world that it was put on, the
play was a branch of Cummings's satirical poetry, which added
up to a glowing example of the level of scorn for capitalism
that could be attained by someone living on a trust fund. In the
cover portrait of his 1954 *Collected Poems* (I had an imported
American copy, obtained God knows how) you could see anti-
capitalist defiance in the tilt of his nostrils, although his open-
necked shirt looked expensive.

In his shorter satirical poems Cummings was usually reined
in by his sense of form and his gift for rhythm (the two qual-
ities are nearly always closely connected, whoever the poet):
and his blazing radical remarks, aided by a knack for comic
timing, got into your head even when he was praising the

Communists, who, had he been in Russia, would have instantly locked him up merely because of his incurable habit of questioning authority.

Some of Cummings's satirical poems have stayed good, but the true paradox of his artistic personality is that some of the passion-soaked romantic arias have lasted even better. The one cited has every possible semantic extravagance right down to the would-be clincher of a final line. But going mad for the loved one is the whole idea of the poem, so every sign of nutty extravagance takes the argument forward, with such an impetus that 'the snow carefully everywhere descending' (a line I loved even though I had never yet seen snow) counts plausibly as a moment of rest. This is the moment to admit, or indeed insist, that Cummings, when he wasn't wasting his time and ours by spreading shattered words all over the page like a burst bag of Alphabetti spaghetti, had a bewitching touch with his rhythms, to the extent that he could advance or retard them at will. The tricks look weak only when the words fall into place too easily from the neck of his cliché-bag.

It must be remembered, however – aspiring oratorical poets are advised to remember this message in letters of fire – that when the volume of pronouncement is raised the reader's acuteness of perception is sharpened. So you really can't say, for example, that you don't know what it is about your beloved that opens and closes. With poetry, absurdity is the chief danger of any deliberate upping of the level of extravagance.

When you command your audience to share your exaltation, they had better go on finding you modestly normal deep down. Shouting through the microphones on the podium is out of fashion – partly, it should be said, because a few writers like Cummings woke up to the fact that they had been foolish about the strutting certainties of any brand of totalitarianism even if it purported to be at war with privilege, and they found their humility again even though, blessedly, they were not shy by nature.

crackup in barcelona

among the bleached skeletons of the olive-trees
stirs a bitter wind
and maxi my friend from the mariahilfer strasse
importunately questions a steely sky
his eyes are two holes made by a dirty finger
in the damp blotting paper of his face
the muscular tissues stretched tautly across the
   scaffolding of bone
are no longer responsive to the factory siren
and never again will the glandular secretions react
to the ragtime promptings of the palais-de-danse
and I am left balanced on Capricorn
the knife-edge tropic between anxiety and regret
while the racing editions are sold at the gates of football
   grounds
and maxi lies on a bare catalan hillside
knocked off the tram by a fascist conductor
who misinterpreted a casual glance.

———

OSBERT LANCASTER'S BRILLIANT LITTLE MONOGRAPH
Drayneflete Revealed features a long line of artistically minded
males of the de Vere-Tipple family. When we reach the middle

of the twentieth century, Guillaume de Vere-Tipple changes his name to 'Bill Tipple' in order to spiritually align himself with the anti-Francoist forces in Spain. In a flash of inspiration, Bill Tipple writes the Spanish Civil War poem with everything. 'crackup in barcelona' doesn't miss a trick. It even remembers to make the first capital letter lower case, so as to get into the revolutionary trend.

Most of the English poets who got themselves mixed up in the Spanish Civil War (notably Auden and Spender) didn't mind being classified as left-wing, because Stalin's role in the conflict had not yet revealed itself to be inimical to freedom. Lancaster was one of those writers who found themselves classified as right-wing simply because they could see through to the dogmatic core of left-wing posturing. He didn't mind, however, bringing in a few ruthless tactics. The bit at the end where the fascist conductor knocks Maxi off the tram is a clear hit at the supposedly homosexual inclinations of the left-wing poets. It's unfair, perhaps, but very funny. Lancaster himself, of course, was so butch that his tweed jacket could have been an air-raid shelter for foxes.

The Sunlight on the Garden

LOUIS MACNEICE
1936

The sunlight on the garden
Hardens and grows cold,
We cannot cage the minute
Within its nets of gold;
When all is told
We cannot beg for pardon.

Our freedom as free lances
Advances towards its end;
The earth compels, upon it
Sonnets and birds descend;
And soon, my friend,
We shall have no time for dances.

The sky was good for flying
Defying the church bells
And every evil iron
Siren and what it tells:
The earth compels,
We are dying, Egypt, dying

And not expecting pardon,
Hardened in heart anew,
But glad to have sat under
Thunder and rain with you,

And grateful too
For sunlight on the garden.

LOUIS MACNEICE, WHO LOVED THE NOTION OF 'THINGS being various', was brilliantly equipped to write the poem that takes in everything, but he also had a knack for divine simplicity. 'The Sunlight on the Garden' is about as simple as he could, or wanted, to be. In fact there is a virtuoso technical trick: there are endings of lines that rhyme with the beginning of the next line, a hard flourish to bring off.

But generally he is striving here to make seemingly plain statements. Even the quotation from *Antony and Cleopatra*, 'We are dying, Egypt, dying', makes more of the cadence than it does of the characters. This was the first poem by MacNeice I ever learned. I went on from his razzle-dazzle short lyrics to the more stately layout of the longer poems.

Like most poets, MacNeice was better at saying goodbye than saying hello. Even in 'The Sunlight on the Garden', the riot of colour is mainly about the flowers fading, rather than growing. I spent years wondering how to borrow, for a book title, his beautiful line in the poem 'Birmingham' about 'the fading zone / Of the west' but the main problem about stealing it is that modern history is much more marked, in my view, by the fading zone of the east.

Another MacNeice lyric that I learned by heart was 'Meeting Point', the one about two lovers keeping a tryst in a cafe, but the plot line of the poem might as well be *Brief Encounter*. These lovers fled away into the storm? These lovers haven't got a prayer? For all we know, these lovers got married and had six children. But we tend to suspect that they haven't got a chance. It was the way MacNeice was. Pretending to be a loser, he worked at self-destruction as if it was an occupation. Yet as a lyric poet he had everything, starting with the indispensable knack of finding the melody already there, in the words.

There are some who believe that MacNeice's poem 'Snow' is one of the best poems ever written in the last or any other century. They have a point. It goes like this:

> The room was suddenly rich and the great bay-window was
> Spawning snow and pink roses against it
> Soundlessly collateral and incompatible:
> World is suddener than we fancy it.

> World is crazier and more of it than we think,
> Incorrigibly plural. I peel and portion
> A tangerine and spit the pips and feel
> The drunkenness of things being various.

> And the fire flames with a bubbling sound for world
> Is more spiteful and gay than one supposes –
> On the tongue on the eyes on the ears in the palms of
>   one's hands –
> There is more than glass between the snow and the
>   huge roses.

I meant to quote only a bit but couldn't stop. Really, even most of his longer poems are too short: he could pack so much in. His long poem *Autumn Journal* would be less effective if he had not known how to keep things tight. *Autumn Journal*, with its teeming variety, remains one of the greatest creations of Thirties poetry, although later he rather blotted his copybook with *Autumn Sequel*, an utter dud. (Fatally he chose *terza rima* for a form, and then, feeling starved for rhymes, took refuge in half-rhyme, giving an effect, unusual for him, of scrabbling for inspiration.) Poets should always be careful when following up on a success; maybe the essence of the second poem is already there in the flavour of the first.

In the winter, when my gallstones were killing me and the usually crackerjack ambulance crew had decided to call in at Vladivostok before they got to my place, I found that a quiet interiorised recital of 'The Sunlight on the Garden' diminished the pain, and that a silent performance of 'Snow' staved off the rest. I won't say that I was found to be smiling when the ambulance finally showed up, but I certainly looked a bit less as if the world were coming to an end.

Missing Dates

WILLIAM EMPSON

1937

Slowly the poison the whole blood stream fills.
It is not the effort nor the failure tires.
The waste remains, the waste remains and kills.

It is not your system or clear sight that mills
Down small to the consequence a life requires;
Slowly the poison the whole blood stream fills.

They bled an old dog dry yet the exchange rills
Of young dog blood gave but a month's desires;
The waste remains, the waste remains and kills.

It is the Chinese tombs and the slag-hills
Usurp the soil, and not the soil retires.
Slowly the poison the whole blood stream fills.

Not to have fire is to be a skin that shrills.
The complete fire is death. From partial fires
The waste remains, the waste remains and kills.

It is the poems you have lost, the ills
From missing dates, at which the heart expires.
Slowly the poison the whole blood stream fills.
The waste remains, the waste remains and kills.

OF THE COMPARATIVELY SMALL HOARD OF POEMS BY William Empson, the one with the best first line ('And now she cleans her teeth into the lake') hasn't quite enough imagistic splendour to follow up on that fabulous idea. This villanelle, on the other hand, ends very strongly with the line that has been set ringing by its repetition throughout the poem. But now, at the last, it connects up, thereby gaining extra force. Empson was really a miniaturist and this poem is a whole treatise in little.

Turn to one of his prose treatises (*Seven Types of Ambiguity* remains a current book) and you can see he was a mighty linguistic analyst. Whether his poems were suitable vehicles for mighty linguistic analysis, however, remains a nagging question. Personally I wanted to know who she was, the woman who cleaned her teeth into the lake: was she a young lady of Cambridge, of the type whose amatory enthusiasm helped to get Empson sent down from the university, or was she a Miss Froy-type dowager British secret agent, an ancient stranger on a train? Instead of expatiating on her, as it were, Empson sends the poem off somewhere else.

In 'Missing Dates', the villanelle that ends so well, the starting line is, in my view, a bit of a fizzer. Why is it written backwards? 'Slowly the poison the whole blood stream fills' sounds like a translation from one of those Germanic languages which the verb at the end of the sentence place. The question becomes doubly relevant if you think, as I do, that 'rills' is a far-fetched rhyme.

Nevertheless he got the backward-stepping line into the reader's head, and from there into the language, in which the word 'Empsonian' came to mean not just arcane imagery but the quirky syntax of compression. That latter quality seems to have been one of his principal aims. Technically capable of every rhythmic trick up to and including the iambic line crammed with trochees and spondees ('Stars how much further from me fill my night'), he wanted to pack things tight, and sometimes he packed them so tight that the suitcase burst open, raining used socks and underpants onto the head of Miss Froy where she sat below, planning her exit from the train so that she could dart away to save Europe.

Across from her sat Empson, filling his notebook with ideas for his new treatise, *Six Types of Ambigu—* wait a second, *Seven Types of Ambiguity*. The clue to Empson might well be there, in the pre-war-to-post-war steadily growing thirst for mysteries that were merely puzzles, instead of questions of life and death.

Elsewhere I have told the story of how, on a reading night in the Cambridge Union, I helped Empson recite a couple of his own poems – he had dined too well earlier in the evening – and he rewarded me with access to a half-full packet of crisps that must have been in his pocket since the Munich Conference. He was a great man, but the poems are hit and miss because of their deadly double concern to disguise meaning as thoroughly as they reveal it. Yet their flavour is unforgettable: the heady tang of a brilliant mind at play. He remains, to this day, the only Cambridge genius who never split an atom, saved Britain from the German U-boat offensive, solved the structure of DNA or indeed did anything except take words apart with the extra authority conferred by the fact that he knew quite a lot about putting them together.

Except for that one damned line: 'Slowly the poison fills the whole bloodstream' would have done the job, at the small price of ending the line with a spondee; but when I pointed this out to my wife she started patting my forehead with a cool flannel.

September 1, 1939

W.H. AUDEN

1939

I sit in one of the dives
On Fifty-second Street
Uncertain and afraid
As the clever hopes expire
Of a low dishonest decade:
Waves of anger and fear
Circulate over the bright
And darkened lands of the earth,
Obsessing our private lives;
The unmentionable odour of death
Offends the September night.

Accurate scholarship can
Unearth the whole offence
From Luther until now
That has driven a culture mad,
Find what occurred at Linz,
What huge imago made
A psychopathic god:
I and the public know
What all schoolchildren learn,
Those to whom evil is done
Do evil in return.

Exiled Thucydides knew
All that a speech can say
About Democracy,
And what dictators do,
The elderly rubbish they talk
To an apathetic grave;
Analysed all in his book,
The enlightenment driven away,
The habit-forming pain,
Mismanagement and grief:
We must suffer them all again.

Into this neutral air
Where blind skyscrapers use
Their full height to proclaim
The strength of Collective Man,
Each language pours its vain
Competitive excuse:
But who can live for long
In an euphoric dream;
Out of the mirror they stare,
Imperialism's face
And the international wrong.

Faces along the bar
Cling to their average day:
The lights must never go out,
The music must always play,
All the conventions conspire
To make this fort assume

The furniture of home;
Lest we should see where we are,
Lost in a haunted wood,
Children afraid of the night
Who have never been happy or good.

The windiest militant trash
Important Persons shout
Is not so crude as our wish:
What mad Nijinsky wrote
About Diaghilev
Is true of the normal heart;
For the error bred in the bone
Of each woman and each man
Craves what it cannot have,
Not universal love
But to be loved alone.

From the conservative dark
Into the ethical life
The dense commuters come,
Repeating their morning vow;
'I will be true to the wife,
I'll concentrate more on my work,'
And helpless governors wake
To resume their compulsory game:
Who can release them now,
Who can reach the deaf,
Who can speak for the dumb?

All I have is a voice
To undo the folded lie,
The romantic lie in the brain
Of the sensual man-in-the-street
And the lie of Authority
Whose buildings grope the sky:
There is no such thing as the State
And no one exists alone;
Hunger allows no choice
To the citizen or the police;
We must love one another or die.

Defenceless under the night
Our world in stupor lies;
Yet, dotted everywhere,
Ironic points of light
Flash out wherever the Just
Exchange their messages:
May I, composed like them
Of Eros and of dust,
Beleaguered by the same
Negation and despair,
Show an affirming flame.

———

THIS POEM 'SEPTEMBER 1, 1939' WAS ONE OF THE FIRST
two longish poems by Auden that I ever learned by heart. (The
other was 'Lullaby', aka 'Lay Your Sleeping Head, My Love'.) His

narrative verse was easy to memorise not just because it was so often vivid in its imagery but because it always had a conversational swing. It seemed that he could just say it aloud and then write it down, thus building up a neatly simple impetus for when you decided to learn the poem yourself.

Indeed you didn't need to decide. The rhythm just got into your head, and stuck. The iambic trimeter can be the devil to handle – it continually threatens to be over as soon as it's begun – but Auden had the gift of opening his structures up so that the sound could reverberate inside them. 'The unmentionable odour of death' unloads a whole cargo of syllables onto its three beats. On the other hand, a line like 'About Democracy' is as spare as a bone picked clean: you might have to look at it twice to check if it's all there, but then you realise that it is.

What occurred at Linz? It seemed a relevant question. But the answer was really 'nothing remarkable'. Hitler was born there but he was raised without trauma: he never even tortured a cat. Perhaps Auden later realised that it was a silly question, but he had a better reason than that for withdrawing the poem. Eventually he realised that 'We must love one another or die' was merely a clever stroke of rhetoric. He replaced the line with 'We must love one another and die' and then he cancelled the poem altogether, as he did also with several other famous efforts, thereby inflicting what would have been huge losses to his corpus, if not that posterity refused to allow it and restored the missing poems, usually at the insistence of his star student Ed Mendelson.

Auden would take poems out and Mendelson put them back in. It became a branch of literary comedy. Just because some poets have it to burn doesn't mean that they should do much burning. And Auden, in my view, had no right to try expunging what he'd already written in stone. Even a piece of puff pastry like 'Letter to Lord Byron' is there for the ages: eloquence set skipping, the world as a game of hopscotch, the very lilt of playful argument.

Well placed in New York when the war started, Auden stayed right where he was. When the conflict was over he showed up in Europe as a member of the American Strategic Bombing Survey, and made himself unpopular with some of his British hosts by suggesting that they had had an easy war. They hadn't, of course. They didn't stop admiring his poems, but I knew at least one distinguished writer (it was Anthony Powell) who went to some lengths to avoid saying his name.

If I was true to my heart, 'Lay Your Sleeping Head' would have been my first choice, because the girls liked hearing it, even when they had no intention of snuggling up to a scruffy poetry fan. It's fabulous; one line after another chipping away at a bar of gold. When the news arrived that the poem had been written for a boy, the girls still liked the poem but the scruffy poetry fan rather went off it. Later on I got sensible again.

Gone to Report

BRIAN HOWARD
1940

For twenty-one years he remained, faithful and lounging
There, under the last tree, at the end of the charming
    evening street.
His flask was always full for the unhappy, rich, or bold;
He could always tell you where you wanted to go, what
    you wanted to be told,
And during all the dear twenty-one years he remained
    exactly twenty-one years old.
His eyes were the most honest of all, his smile the most
    naturally sweet.

Many, many trusted him who trusted no one. Many
    extremely clever
Persons will kill themselves unless they find him. They
    search
Sparkling with fear, through the whole quarter. They
    even enter the Church.
Crowds, across all Europe, are beginning to feel they've
    been left in the lurch.
But it's worse than that. It's something they couldn't tell
    anyone, ever.

He's abandoned his post because he was the greatest of
    all informers,

And now he's gone to report. He never had a moment's
leisure.
He was paid by so many powers that one shakes with
shame
To think of them. Time, the Army and Navy, Pain and
Blame,
The Police, the Family, and Death. No one will escape.
He got every name.
And he wasn't at all what he said he was. Mr. Pleasure.

———

APART FROM THIS POEM, BRIAN HOWARD ACCOMPLISHED
next to nothing. He was a standard-issue British upper-class
wastrel, and was actually used as a very identifiable model for
louche uselessness in Evelyn Waugh's *Brideshead Revisited*,
where he was the prototype for Anthony Blanche, drinking
brandy at a prodigious rate and making a startling appearance
broadcasting fragments of *The Waste Land* through a mega-
phone.

Although a wastrel, Howard was the reverse of stupid. As
Erika Mann later recorded, Howard was among the first
Englishmen to see the evil of the Nazis. At a Nazi rally of 1931
he wasn't fooled by their theatricality and spotted the murderous
anti-Semitism, which years later still wasn't bothering such
other British travellers as the Duke of Windsor. In retrospect he
looks politically prescient but we should be careful when attrib-
uting to him any particular energy. He was at his most
characteristic when wasting time.

Later on, having enrolled in the British army, Howard soon established a glittering reputation for being entirely useless. He distinguished himself by being on the verge of expulsion, if not execution, throughout the conflict. To read an account of his military exploits is to wonder why the Germans didn't win the war in the first week. If only he had established a compensatory reputation as a writer. Alas, little he wrote remains apart from this one poem.

And a fabulous poem it is: kinetic, vivid, chargingly rhythmic, electrically charged. It has a cunningly disguised progressive structure by which the reader only gradually realises that the narrator is talking about himself – or rather he is talking about his own *alter ego*. In Howard's case the *alter ego* was actually himself. It is one of the great poems of spiritual dissipation, and nobody is likely to approve of it. But any other poet will acknowledge the perfect dramatic timing with which the last line unfolds. He is like a music-hall performer who climaxes his solo act by having the lights turned up instead of down.

War of Nerves

FREDERIC PROKOSCH
1940

Some lie on the tennis lawn, some on the edge of a brook,
Others walk through landscapes with a compass or a book,
A few sit in the arbour, studying the deformities of words:
Grief carries them away
As they pore from day to day
Over old Scottish legends or the markings of rare birds.

The mannequin sips at her green liqueur glass on the beach,
The student crosses the plaza preparing a brilliant speech;
The ballerina plunges the calming needle into her arm,
Night after hopeless night
Stabbing the real delight,
Stabbing whatever once was real and plentiful and warm.

Doomed by a stray encounter on a midnight train,
One has ended by suddenly putting a bullet in his brain,
One spends his nights listening to Beethoven and Brahms,
And one, the golden-haired
At whom the ladies stared
Is growing bald and fatuous under the windless palms.

Green, iridescent flies gather upon the rosy fruit,
The black-snouted telephone is an emblem of pursuit,
The postman's knock becomes a prelude to disaster;
The boats in the little bay

Move slowly, slowly away
While the delicate mad wheels are turning faster and faster.

Marconi, Marx, Miss Garbo, Dr Goebbels and Dr Freud
Huddle like assassins over the staggering void.
Faces illumined by the roving flames, they move
Their devastating glance,
Their empty lips and hands
Exquisitely to and fro in the mimicries of love.

The poplar leaves uplifted and silvered by the wind,
The cows grazing under the willows at the river's bend,
Yes, even the salmon leaping heavenward up the stream
Move inward through our eyes,
Marvellously they rise,
Characters in the knifing, bottomless crisis of a dream.

Patiently the delta mutters, the estuaries sigh,
Under the August heaven the five great continents lie,
And somewhere as the starlight touches the mountain sheep
Under their hood of ice
The waters well and rise,
Waiting to calm the sleepy and to bless the still asleep.

———

As with Brian Howard, Frederic Prokosch's barely traceable career gives the impression that he couldn't concentrate on anything for more than ten minutes at a time. Like many a mystery man, he overestimated the fascination of his mystery, which in retrospect looks merely tedious, like the itinerary of a tramp. But his technical dexterity redeemed everything, apart from the occasional clumsiness, which might or might not have been deliberate. Even at this distance in time, is he still trying to get our attention? Anyway, 'ice' and 'rise' do not rhyme, and neither do 'glance' and 'hands'. He probably knew that, and just bunged the blunders in anyway, correctly assuming that his chosen form has unstoppable impetus. The poem is a wreck, but a great wreck. The image in the second stanza which gives us the ballerina shooting up is a beautiful horror-show framed as a cameo, and 'Waiting to calm the sleepy and to bless the still asleep' is a closing line fit for angels.

Canoe

KEITH DOUGLAS
1940

Well, I am thinking this may be my last
summer, but cannot lose even a part
of pleasure in the old-fashioned art
of idleness. I cannot stand aghast

at whatever doom hovers in the background:
while grass and buildings and the somnolent river,
who know they are allowed to last forever,
exchange between them the whole subdued sound

of this hot time. What sudden fearful fate
can deter my shade wandering next year
from a return? Whistle and I will hear
and come again another evening, when this boat

travels with you alone toward Iffley:
as you lie looking up for thunder again,
this cool touch does not betoken rain;
it is my spirit that kisses your mouth lightly.

———

KEITH DOUGLAS WAS BORN TO BE A CLASSICAL POET, SO
it should not be surprising that his beautifully poised poem

'Canoe' was written quite early in his career, before he went off to war and wrote the poems that would make him famous. Yet 'Canoe' is still prodigious for the concentrated pathos of its landscape, the Oxford setting so very like Virgil's *lugentes campos*, the weeping fields. The moment that melts my eyes is towards the end, when the young woman in the canoe is pictured as making her journey alone in the future, because the narrator will not be with her. At that point, the story is already clinched; he has, we think, foreseen his death, although the poem would have remained powerful even if he had got back, grown old, and died in bed.

But in a poem that is all grace, the supremely gracious moment is yet to come. Suddenly he becomes a ghost – for decades in my memory, until I corrected it against the text, it was always his ghost, and not his 'spirit' – and he 'kisses her mouth lightly.' By then I can hardly breathe for grief. The grief is personal, of course. My father went away to the war; he, too, was fated never to return; and my mother continued her voyage alone. This great poem could have been written about them, and therefore about me.

Looking back, we might think that Keith Douglas set out his stall when he wrote 'Canoe', but we can think that because he did indeed go to war not long afterwards, and did indeed get killed, a loss that is still hard to accept. Compare this poem to 'Vergissmeinnicht', one of the poems he wrote while he was fighting in North Africa, and you get some notion of how the world had changed, from peace to war. (Usually at this point I would quote a fragment, but in this case the pieces fly back together when you try to pull them apart. This is the whole poem.)

Three weeks gone and the combatants gone
returning over the nightmare ground
we found the place again, and found
the soldier sprawling in the sun.

The frowning barrel of his gun
overshadowing. As we came on
that day, he hit my tank with one
like the entry of a demon.

Look. Here in the gunpit spoil
the dishonoured picture of his girl
who has put: *Steffi. Vergissmeinnicht.*
in a copybook gothic script.

We see him almost with content,
abased, and seeming to have paid
and mocked at by his own equipment
that's hard and good when he's decayed.

But she would weep to see today
how on his skin the swart flies move;
the dust upon the paper eye
and the burst stomach like a cave.

For here the lover and killer are mingled
who had one body and one heart.
And death who had the soldier singled
has done the lover mortal hurt.

'Vergissmeinnicht' is a complete and completely unforgettable study in the contemplation of death. The death has happened to a German soldier, and Douglas, standing over the corpse, is realising that the soldier once had a life. *Vergissmeinnicht* is the German word for forget-me-not, and Douglas must know that, as he reads Steffi's letter. But the dead German soldier will not forget her only because he won't remember anything. He's gone, and not long afterwards Keith Douglas was gone too.

Douglas might seem to have been born for a war, but he was in fact born to die in one. He spent the earliest part of his war in the Western Desert. Typically, after being in the heart of the action in Africa, including the Battle of El Alamein, he contrived his return to Europe only because he wanted to not miss D-Day. Quite a lot of British poets spent the war looking for one safe billet after another, but Douglas was of the type to head towards maximum danger. This proclivity would have had less devastating results if he had been less talented: as things happened, Britain lost a poet who might have changed the literary future. In command of a tank, he was killed in Normandy not long after D-Day, at the age of twenty-four, and one could say that a whole path to the poetic future was blocked from that moment.

Stern of jaw and tanned of skin, Keith Douglas had a steely exterior and a universal sympathy. He was the complete fighting male. 'Simplify me when I'm dead' was a key line of one of his great poems, and unfortunately that's exactly what happened, because today he is remembered more for being promising than for being a promise fulfilled. But in fact he was already all there.

Naming of Parts

HENRY REED
1942

Today we have naming of parts. Yesterday,
We had daily cleaning. And tomorrow morning,
We shall have what to do after firing. But today,
Today we have naming of parts. Japonica
Glistens like coral in all of the neighbouring gardens,
    And today we have naming of parts.

This is lower sling swivel. And this
Is the upper sling swivel, whose use you will see,
When you are given your slings. And this is the piling swivel,
Which in your case you have not got. The branches
Hold in the gardens their silent, eloquent gestures,
    Which in our case we have not got.

This is the safety-catch, which is always released
With an easy flick of the thumb. And please do not let me
See anyone using his finger. You can do it quite easy
If you have any strength in your thumb. The blossoms
Are fragile and motionless, never letting anyone see
    Any of them using their finger.

And this you can see is the bolt. The purpose of this
Is to open the breech, as you see. We can slide it
Rapidly backwards and forwards: we call this
Easing the spring. And rapidly backwards and forwards

The early bees are assaulting and fumbling the flowers:
    They call it easing the Spring.

They call it easing the Spring: it is perfectly easy
If you have any strength in your thumb: like the bolt,
And the breech, and the cocking-piece, and the point of
    balance,
Which in our case we have not got; and the
    almond-blossom
Silent in all of the gardens and the bees going backward
    and forwards,
    For today we have naming of parts.

———

HENRY REED'S TRIO OF SHORT LONG POEMS, OR LONG short ones – it went under the general title of *Lessons of the War* – constitutes one of the best literary things that came out of Britain in the Second World War. Since he also wrote 'Chard Whitlow', the best parody of T.S. Eliot (even Eliot thought so) it could be said that Reed, viewed in retrospect, was a massive wartime poetic presence.

In fact he was reluctant to come forward, and, when forced to, would hang around diffidently until the spotlights went off again. His slim collection *A Map of Verona* holds almost all of his poetry that there ever was. But that resonant little wartime trilogy (it unfolds rather like a Flemish altar-piece) persists in being still with us, and the first of its three poems lavishly shows, when recited, what he could do to suit the human voice. Just try not saying it aloud.

The setting is somnolent. (As I learned in National Service, most of your time as a military trainee will be spent waiting.) The instructor's voice is a rude awakening. We presume instantly and correctly that the helpless narrator is on the receiving end of it. When the japonica glistens in the neighbouring gardens, it is just a case of the trainee ransacking his memories of a more peaceful life so that he can interrupt and civilise, if only in his own mind, the instructor's graceless tirade, which is practised and eloquent (he has taken dozens of classes like this one) but no more polished than a builder's mallet. Reed's narrator – clearly an educated gent, a civilian – is out of place: but then almost everyone on our side of the war was, whatever their social origin. It was the enemy who had the born soldiers.

So we were lucky to win. The second poem in the trilogy provides sufficient sidelight on the first one to make the point. In 'Judging Distances' the same sort of instructor (perhaps the very same one) is barking away while the counterpoint, this time, is provided by a pair of lovers in the distance. The counter-theme seems unlikely. When I did my own open-air courting, I was usually careful to stay well away from any groups of soldiers sitting out in the mulga listening to a lecture, and later on, when I was in the army and doing the listening, I never saw a single pair of lovers anywhere in the vicinity.

But the idea supplies a reliably recurring frisson: if there truly was a brace of lovers out there in the landscape and apparently in the process of getting it on, the instructor probably would emphasise the importance of not jumping to conclusions: '. . . a pair of what appear to be humans / Appear to be loving.' Anyway, Reed was funny, which hardly any poets are, even by intention. When I think of his superbly Eliotesque line at the heart of 'Chard Whitlow', I still smile:

As we get older we do not get any younger . . .

No, we don't.

Green, Green is El Aghir

NORMAN CAMERON

C. 1943

Sprawled on the bags and crates in the rear of the truck,
I was gummy-mouthed from the sun and the dust of
   the track;
And the two Arab soldiers I'd taken on as hitch-hikers
At a torrid petrol-dump, had been there on their hunkers
Since early morning. I said, in a kind of French
'On m'a dit, qu'il y a une belle source d'eau fraiche.
Plus loin, à El Aghir.'
                     It was eighty more kilometres.
Until round a corner we heard a splashing of waters,
And there, in a green, dark street, was a fountain with
   two facets,
Discharging both ways, from full-throated faucets,
Into basins, thence into troughs and thence into brooks.
Our Negro corporal driver slammed his brakes,
And we yelped and leapt from the truck and went at
   the double
To fill our bidons and bottles and drink and dabble.
Then, swollen with water, we went to an inn for wine.
The Arabs came, too, though their faith might have
   stood between.
'After all,' they said, 'it's a boisson,' without contrition.

Green, green is El Aghir. It has a railway station,
And the wealth of its soil has borne many another fruit,

A mairie, a school and an elegant Salle de Fêtes.
Such blessings, as I remarked, in effect, to the waiter,
Are added unto them that have plenty of water.

———

ROBERT GRAVES SAID THAT NORMAN CAMERON WAS A
neglected poet, and thereby revived Cameron's reputation for a
moment. Graves is still remembered, and ought to be, for his
memoir *Good-Bye to All That*, not to mention the *Claudius*
books; but his poetry, in my opinion, by now adds up to a back
number. Cameron, now almost entirely forgotten, was by far the
better poet, and the main reason for Cameron's supremacy is the
quality of his war poetry. Cameron captured the North Africa
campaign with the brilliant device of stressing the tourist aspect,
so that this poem 'Green, Green is El Aghir' is like a series of
glossy magazine photographs, with a smart commentary.

The smartness is underlined by the flash succession of near-
rhymes and half-rhymes. The structure couldn't be trickier, and
yet at the end we see why the trickiness has been structural – it
leads up to a beautiful simplicity. The use of French is just ele-
vated enough to remind you that he is speaking it with fair
fluency as a second language: a little better than you might have
done yourself, perhaps.

What is he doing there, bashing around in the desert? It was
a hard enough question for the Afrika Korps to answer, let alone
an English gentleman. It was history. It was the war. In another
poem, his evocation of 'a rich, two-way traffic of deserters'
appears to give us a taste of the only saving grace the war offers.
But humour won't save a single life.

Strangely enough, not even the poems of Keith Douglas capture the war in the desert with quite the intensity of this poem by Cameron. Like all his work, it breathes his fastidious elegance. The British officers of the Long Range Desert Group were all as chic as male fashion models for a post-war copy of *Vogue d'Hommes*. Somehow that fact only multiplies the power of an apparently effortless poem which reminds us that the war in the desert, like war anywhere, isn't elegant at all.

The Silken Tent

ROBERT FROST

1942

She is as in a field a silken tent
At midday when the sunny summer breeze
Has dried the dew and all its ropes relent,
So that in guys it gently sways at ease,
And its supporting central cedar pole,
That is its pinnacle to heavenward
And signifies the sureness of the soul,
Seems to owe naught to any single cord,
But strictly held by none, is loosely bound
By countless silken ties of love and thought
To every thing on earth the compass round,
And only by one's going slightly taut
In the capriciousness of summer air
Is of the slightest bondage made aware.

———

THOUGH EXTREMELY COMPLICATED IN ITS GRAMMATICAL
structure, Robert Frost's poem 'The Silken Tent' is divinely
simple, and almost impossible to get wrong, except for the
famous young American academic who thought that 'guys'
meant the blokes, or the chaps as the British would say, who
were putting the tent up. So the poem's real problem is not lack
of clarity, but too much of it. It all looks so simple: as indeed the

tent does. But what is holding it up? Tension, gravity, the universe, eternity? The questions begin to flow endlessly. Frost's strength was that he knew they were flowing: he was a rider on the storm.

This is the supreme Frost poem, if you want to sum him up. Judiciousness of language mixes with a limitless capacity to set fancy flying. Look above all at the way the word 'capriciousness' is brought in. Notice also that the poem is a single sentence. It reminds me of that wooden puzzle we used to get in our Christmas stockings. A polished wooden sphere not much bigger than a golf-ball could be disassembled in a matter of seconds into a stack of component pieces but putting them back together again took hours and sometimes resulted in sobbing hysterics. This poem is like that.

The Death of the Ball Turret Gunner

RANDALL JARRELL

1945

From my mother's sleep I fell into the State,
And I hunched in its belly till my wet fur froze.
Six miles from earth, loosed from its dream of life,
I woke to black flak and the nightmare fighters.
When I died they washed me out of the turret with a hose.

RANDALL JARRELL, THOUGH ENROLLED IN THE AMERICAN air force, was too old for combat in the Second World War, but with this little poem, about the air battle over Europe, he proved that poets could sometimes see the whole picture from a distance. In a poem whose every phrase deserves close study, the reader shouldn't miss the womb-like nature of the ball turret: it clasped and cradled the gunner very closely.

Jarrell's job was to instruct young bomber crews. The gunner in the poem might well have been one of his pupils. 'Wet fur' reminds us of an animal, but we should remember that his leather jacket probably had a fur collar; although probably we are meant to be thinking of a human baby. Like the foetus in the womb, the ball-turret gunner was often upside down. 'Six miles from earth' is rather higher than the American bombers could usually go, but there is nothing unreal about 'the nightmare fighters', especially since the American bombers flew by daylight, so the gunners could see what was coming.

The last line is one of the most famous lines in the whole library of Second World War poetry, and it was written by a man who was never shot at; a reminder that the imagination is the most powerful thing in reality. In modern times, Jarrell was probably America's best critic of poetry. His collection of essays, *Poetry and the Age*, is still thought of, correctly, as a benchmark book: one of the rare cases of a poet writing an essential book about the art that has consumed his life.

Dedication

On Editing Scott Fitzgerald's Papers

EDMUND WILSON

1945

Scott, your last fragments I arrange tonight,
Assigning commas, setting accents right,
As once I punctuated, spelled and trimmed
When, passing in a Princeton spring—how
   dimmed
By this damned quarter-century and more!—
You left your *Shadow Laurels* at my door.
That was a drama webbed of dreams: the scene
A shimmering beglamored bluish-green
Soiled Paris wineshop; the sad hero one
Who loved applause but had his life alone;
Who fed on drink for weeks; forgot to eat,
"Worked feverishly," nourished on defeat
A lyric pride, and lent a lyric voice
To all the tongueless knavish tavern boys,
The liquor-ridden, the illiterate;
Got stabbed one midnight by a tavern-mate—
Betrayed, but self-betrayed by stealthy sins—
And faded to the sound of violins.

Tonight, in this dark long Atlantic gale,
I set in order such another tale,
While tons of wind that take the world for scope
Rock blackened waters where marauders grope

Our blue and bathed-in Massachusetts ocean;
The Cape shakes with the depth-bomb's dumbed
    concussion;
And guns can interrupt me in these rooms,
Where now I seek to breathe again the fumes
Of iridescent drinking-dens, retrace
The bright hotels, regain the eager pace
You tell of . . . Scott, the bright hotels turn bleak;
The pace limps or stamps; the wines are weak;
The horns and violins come faint tonight.
A rim of darkness that devours light
Runs like the wall of flame that eats the land;
Blood, brain and labor pour into the sand;
And here, among our comrades of the trade,
Some buzz like husks, some stammer, much afraid,
Some mellowly give tongue and join the drag
Like hounds that bay the bounding anise-bag,
Some swallow darkness and sit hunched and dull,
The stunned beast's stupor in the monkey-skull.

I climbed, a quarter-century and more
Played out, the college steps, unlatched my door,
And, creature strange to college, found you there:
The pale skin, hard green eyes, and yellow hair—
Intently pinching out before a glass
Some pimples left by parties at the Nass;
Nor did you stop abashed, thus pocked and
    blotched,
But kept on peering while I stood and watched.
Tonight, from days more distant now, we find,
Than holidays in France were, left behind,

Than spring of graduation from the fall
That saw us grubbing below City Hall,
Through storm and darkness, Time's contrary stream,
There glides amazingly your mirror's beam—
To bring before me still, glazed mirror-wise,
The glitter of the hard and emerald eyes.
The cornea tough, the aqueous chamber cold,
Those glassy optic bulbs that globe and hold—
They pass their image on to what they mint,
To blue ice or light buds attune their tint,
And leave us, to turn over, iris-fired,
Not the great Ritz-sized diamond you desired
But jewels in a handful, lying loose:
Flawed amethysts; the moonstone's milky blues;
Chill blues of pale transparent tourmaline;
Opals of shifty yellow, chartreuse green,
Wherein a vein vermilion flees and flickers—
Tight phials of the spirit's light mixed liquors;
Some tinsel zircons, common turquoise; but
Two emeralds, green and lucid, one half-cut,
One cut consummately—both take their place
In Letters' most expensive Cartier case.

And there I have set them out for final show,
And come to the task's dead-end, and dread to know
Those eyes struck dark, dissolving in a wrecked
And darkened world, that gleam of intellect
That spilled into the spectrum of tune, taste,
Scent, color, living speech, is gone, is lost;
And we must dwell among the ragged stumps,
With owls digesting mice to dismal lumps

Of skin and gristle, monkeys scared by thunder,
Great buzzards that descend to grab the plunder.
And I, your scraps and sketches sifting yet,
Can never thus revive one sapphire jet,
However close I look, however late,
But only spell and point and punctuate.

———

WILSON WAS NOT ONLY A GREAT CRITIC, BUT A TECHNICALLY accomplished poet in his own right. He was not notably a generous man in his enthusiasms, but in this dedicatory poem he gives a dazzling ceremonial farewell to his friend F. Scott Fitzgerald. Some of Wilson's poetic ideas could be enchantingly fanciful. 'Chill blues of pale transparent tourmaline': the rhythmically packed line is like a pig-skin hold-all full of neatly folded cashmere sweaters. He was a great appreciator of poetry on the technical level. And there can be no doubt about the grace of his mind – or anyway, about the poetic part of his mind. In prose he was more fallible. It had taken him an age to figure out that something sinister might be going on in Russia, and the future would reveal that he wasn't sure about the wisdom of America's coming to Britain's aid against Hitler.

But in this fine poem, whole chunks of which I still have by heart, America is already embroiled willy-nilly in the Second World War. Fitzgerald's era is over: he died in 1940, leaving *The Last Tycoon* unfinished. (Wilson was the editor who got the book into shape: by the 'half-cut' emerald he probably means *Tender is the Night*, and by the emerald 'cut consummately' he certainly means *The Great Gatsby*.)

Wilson, however, was only just getting started. He had every right to shape his valediction as if he himself were a venerable figure and would go on being one of those for a long time to come.

In My Craft or Sullen Art

Dylan Thomas
1946

In my craft or sullen art
Exercised in the still night
When only the moon rages
And the lovers lie abed
With all their griefs in their arms,
I labour by singing light
Not for ambition or bread
Or the strut and trade of charms
On the ivory stages
But for the common wages
Of their most secret heart.

Not for the proud man apart
From the raging moon I write
On these spindrift pages
Nor for the towering dead
With their nightingales and psalms
But for the lovers, their arms
Round the griefs of the ages,
Who pay no praise or wages
Nor heed my craft or art.

THE FIRST DYLAN THOMAS POEM I EVER LEARNED BY heart was this one. I can still recite it today, although I still don't know why he thought poetry was a sullen art. How sullen was Andrew Marvell? And 'Fern Hill', which is among Thomas's greatest poems, is a festival. But this poem was one of his biggest performance hits on the American tours in the early '50s, whose alcoholic effects reinforced the pattern that eventually did him in. On the Caedmon LP record, which we played to pieces back there at the Sydney house parties in the late 1950s, he performs it like a tenor who has escaped from the nearest opera house, condemned never to hear an orchestra again, so he must supply his own music from the weight and balance of the words.

Thomas's claim of altruism in conferring his druidic voice on the public looks rather shameless in the light of the fact that the box office boomed, but everyone understood the posture he was striking as the dedicated self-sacrificing bard. The downside of his New York success was that it helped to establish the possibility of drinking himself not just to temporary oblivion but to death.

The poem believably presents his crafty art as an enchantment: he's enchanted and so are we. The bardic posturing was made more noticeable by the microphone, the loudspeakers and the general massed swoon of the women in the audience, who, their minds scrambled by the charm of his voice, gazed upon his bulbous form and found it as muscular as Hercules. And indeed there is something heroic about his cadences. The first time I heard him recite the poem on the Caedmon record I found his voice divine. I briefly made the almost-fatal mistake of copying it in real life. Australians don't cope well with being addressed in heroic tones.

The success of the poem does not depend just on the voice, however. 'Nor for the towering dead' is pieced into the general scheme with an impact shattering enough to make you forget that the nightingales and psalms are a strained and indeed strange yoking of decorative properties. But the impetus is unstoppable – he has plenty of power in reserve for the line that ultimately brings it to a halt.

He knows very well, of course, that everybody in the hall is heeding him. There are people heeding him in the nearby subway. His was a voice in a million. But in fact some of his greatest poems actually were written during long hours at the desk and not just mumbled in his sleep. It wasn't discipline that he lacked; it was dignity. Equipped with the lightning reflexes of a champion sponge, he could borrow money from people on a passing train. When he put the bite on people who knew him, some of them were enraged, but then they remembered that they had made a contribution to an angelic trajectory:

> The ball I threw when playing in the park
> Has not yet reached the ground.

Fancy being able to say you'd written that.

From The Avenue Bearing the Initial of Christ into the New World

Galway Kinnell

1951

The Downtown Talmud Torah
Blosztein's Cutrate Bakery
Areceba Panataria Hispano
Peanuts Dried Fruits Nuts & Canned Goods
Productos Tropicales
Appetizing Herring Candies Nuts
Nathan Kugler Chicken Store Fresh Killed Daily
Little Rose Restaurant
Rubinstein the Hatter Mens Boys Hats Caps Furnishings
J Herrmann Dealer in All Kinds of Bottles
Natural Bloom Cigars
Blony Bubblegum
Mueren las Cucarachas Super Potente Garantizada de
    Matar las Cucarachas mas Resistentes
Wenig סעבוח
G Schnee Stairbuilder
Everyouth la Original Loción Eterna Juventud
    Satisfacción Dinero Devuelto
Happy Days Bar & Grill

Through dust-stained windows over storefronts
Curtains drawn aside, onto the Avenue
Thronged with Puerto Ricans, Negroes, Jews,
Baby carriages stuffed with groceries and babies,

The old women peer, blessed damozels
Sitting up there young forever in the cockroached rooms,
Eating fresh-killed chicken, productos tropicales,
Appetizing herring, canned goods, nuts;
They puff out smoke from Natural Bloom cigars
And one day they puff like Blony Bubblegum.
Across the square skies with faces in them
Pigeons skid, crashing into the brick.
From a rooftop a boy fishes at the sky.
Around him a flock of pigeons fountains,
Blown down and swirling up again, seeking the sky.
From the skyview they must seem
A whirlwind on a desert seeking itself;
Here they break from the rim of buildings
Without rank in the blue military cemetery sky.
A red kite wriggles like a tadpole
Into the sky beyond them, crosses
The sun, lays bare its own crossed skeleton.

To fly from this place – to roll
On some bubbly blacktop in the summer,
To run under the rain of pigeon plumes, to be
Tarred, and feathered with birdshit, Icarus,

In Kugler's glass headdown dangling by yellow legs.

**

In the pushcart market, on Sunday,
A crate of lemons discharges light like a battery.

**

The fishmarket closed, the fishes gone into flesh.
The smelts draped on each other, fat with roe,

The marble cod hacked into chunks on the counter,
Butterfishes mouths still open, still trying to eat,
Porgies with receding jaws hinged apart
In a grimace of dejection, as if like cows
They had died under the sledgehammer, perches
In grass-green armor, spotted squeteagues
In the melting ice meek-faced and croaking no more,
Except in the plip plop plip plip in the bucket,
Mud-eating mullets buried in crushed ice,
Tilefishes with scales like chickenfat,
Spanish mackerels, buttercups on the flanks,
Pot-bellied pikes, two-tone flounders
After the long contortion of pushing both eyes
To the brown side that they might look up,
Brown side down, like a laying-on of hands,
As at the oath-taking of an army.

———

GALWAY KINNELL COULD WRITE SHORT POEMS – THERE
are half a dozen collections of them – but as an admirer of
Whitman he must have known that the long poem was his des-
tiny. Anyway, he wrote one. It had the best title ever, *The Avenue
Bearing the Initial of Christ into the New World*, and has
remained his signature work, partly because its background
theme, the destruction of the European Jews, is still with us as
a current event. But the poem is set in New York, not Europe,
and in Kinnell's New York the Jews are very much alive.

At the start of my chosen extract, the Jews are one population
among many, and that, we will later conclude, is part of the

point. Everything is happening in the street, except a parade with banners saying that one racial group should be eliminated. Behind the vividness of the street scene is the capaciousness of a Constitution. For now, however, we are preoccupied with the vivid images.

A red kite wriggles like a tadpole
Into the sky beyond them, crosses
The sun, lays bare its own crossed skeleton.

All of his word pictures, throughout the poem, flare with that magnesium intensity. This is ordinary life being photographed as if its meaning must be captured now, so as to be kept for ever. Try this:

A crate of lemons discharges light like a battery.

And then, finally, this:

two-tone flounders
After the long contortion of pushing both eyes
To the brown side that they might look up,
Brown side down, like a laying-on of hands,
As at the oath-taking of an army.

One self-explanatory perception follows another until we finally get to a perception that needs explaining. Even then, all we have to do is connect the look of the hands with the look of the fish.

New York is the perfect setting because America is the place where the Holocaust could never have happened. Philip Roth sabotaged his otherwise fine novel *The Plot Against America* because for once he took leave of his senses and refused to understand the obvious. In America, ever since Lincoln, no one group of people has plausibly been able to suggest the elimination of another. They can only do it implausibly.

Elsewhere in the poem – which isn't really that enormous, just longer than short – the teeming variety of the city unfolds in all directions, and it could be argued that the destruction of the European Jews is only one of its many themes. But without that event, the poem would never have happened, which is part of Kinnell's point. There is a wound in the world's consciousness, and he has found a way of treating it.

A Bookshop Idyll

KINGSLEY AMIS

C. 1953

Between the gardening and the cookery
   Comes the brief poetry shelf;
By the Nonesuch Donne, a thin anthology
   Offers itself.

Critical, and with nothing else to do,
   I scan the Contents page,
Relieved to find the names are mostly new;
   No one my age.

Like all strangers, they divide by sex:
   Landscape near Parma
Interests a man, so does *The Double Vortex*,
   So does *Rilke and Buddha*.

'I travel, you see', 'I think' and 'I can read'
   These titles seem to say;
But *I Remember You, Love is my Creed,*
   Poem for J.,

The ladies' choice, discountenance my patter
   For several seconds;
From somewhere in this (as in any) matter
   A moral beckons.

Should poets bicycle-pump the human heart
    Or squash it flat?
Man's love is of man's life a thing apart;
    Girls aren't like that.

We men have got love well weighed up; our stuff
    Can get by without it.
Women don't seem to think that's good enough;
    They write about it,

And the awful way their poems lay them open
    Just doesn't strike them.
Women are really much nicer than men:
    No wonder we like them.

Deciding this, we can forget those times
    We sat up half the night
Chockfull of love, crammed with bright thoughts, names,
    rhymes,
    And couldn't write.

———

KINGSLEY AMIS HAD COMIC TIMING IN ALL THINGS, IN whatever genre he practised. Look at the way the deliberately stilted Byronic line 'Man's love is of man's life a thing apart' is undercut straightaway by the superb banality of 'Girls aren't like that.' Very few poets can make you smile that way. But should I be smiling?

I love this poem, though these days many people, perhaps

most people, would argue that I shouldn't. I write as one for whom browsing in a second-hand bookshop has always been one of life's greatest pleasures. I still own a copy of that Nonesuch Donne, bought in identical circumstances. Kingsley Amis often said that poets shouldn't write poems about the arts, but this poem about a bookshop breaks his own rule, because if it's not about literature, what is it about?

Well, it's about women. Though his love of books is obviously genuine, it's also clear, or gets clear, that his love of women is genuine. What makes the poem equivocal, however, is the way he gives women a separate mentality. It's hard to accept now that he was a man of his age. People – not just men – thought this kind of thing then. Barbara Everett, the Oxford-based literary scholar, once wrote articles to prove that Amis was not a male chauvinist after all, but few believed her. They had a point. If Amis in *Lucky Jim* had been any more cruel to Margaret Peel (his caricature of Philip Larkin's mistress Monica Jones) he would have had to be strung up.

'No wonder we like them.' Does he really like them, as opposed to running after them, barking like a dog? I would say that Kingsley Amis's real tenderness for women was proved conclusively by his wonderful novel ('a real fireworks display', the great editor Karl Miller accurately called it) *Take a Girl Like You*, which has a female not just as the novel's centre of morality, but the centre of strength. In the bookshop poem Kingsley Amis is actually playing fast and loose with his own beliefs, which may be what adds the tang of gunpowder to the mixture. Anyone who knew him would smile wryly at the contention of 'no wonder we like them': when a love went sour, even a long-term love, he could be cruelly scornful, but he thought that the way he turned savage only proved how tender he had previously been.

There is no question, in my mind, that Kingsley Amis *was* a male chauvinist. But he was not a misogynist. As a political statement, generalising about the nature of women, the poem is a horror. But is generalising really what it does? Perhaps a better word would be 'specifying'. Isn't it a personal rumination on love? Is the tone scornful about women or is it yearning? Is it smug about the supposed intellectual superiority of men, or is it skewering that idea? The main tone I get from the poem, when I read it now, is the tone of regret – regret, perhaps, that he was ever in a tangle on the subject, he who took such pride in knowing exactly what he thought.

Remembering The 'Thirties

DONALD DAVIE

1953

Hearing one saga, we enact the next.
We please our elders when we sit enthralled;
But then they're puzzled; and at last they're vexed
To have their youth so avidly recalled.

It dawns upon the veterans after all
That what for them were agonies, for us
Are high-brow thrillers, though historical;
And all their feats quite strictly fabulous.

This novel written fifteen years ago,
Set in my boyhood and my boyhood home,
These poems about 'abandoned workings', show
Worlds more remote than Ithaca or Rome.

The Anschluss, Guernica – all the names
At which those poets thrilled or were afraid
For me mean schools and headmasters and games;
And in the process someone is betrayed.

Ourselves perhaps. The Devil for a joke
Might carve his own initials on our desk,
And yet we'd miss the point because he spoke
An idiom too dated, Audenesque.

Ralegh's Guiana also killed his son.
A pretty pickle if we came to see
The tallest story really packed a gun,
The Telemachiad an Odyssey.

2

Even to them the tales were not so true
As not to be ridiculous as well;
The ironmaster met his Waterloo,
But Rider Haggard rode along the fell.

'Leave for Cape Wrath tonight!' They lounged away
On Fleming's trek or Isherwood's ascent.
England expected every man that day
To show his motives were ambivalent.

They played the fool, not to appear as fools
In time's long glass. A deprecating air
Disarmed, they thought, the jeers of later schools;
Yet irony itself is doctrinaire,

And, curiously, nothing now betrays
Their type to time's derision like this coy
Insistence on the quizzical, their craze
For showing Hector was a mother's boy.

A neutral tone is nowadays preferred.
And yet it may be better, if we must,
To praise a stance impressive and absurd
Than not to see the hero for the dust.

For courage is the vegetable king,
The sprig of all ontologies, the weed
That beards the slag-heap with his hectoring,
Whose green adventure is to run to seed.

———

IF DONALD DAVIE HAD WRITTEN EVEN HALF A DOZEN
poems like this he might have dominated his generation, though
he would have needed to keep the range of reference slightly
more restricted. Even today, when everything is on the internet,
readers tend to resent having to search things out. Few readers
would know what the *Telemachiad* is without looking it up, and
by now 'Fleming' would probably be more likely to call up Ian
Fleming, who has attained historic status because of James
Bond, than any other Fleming, although there is, of course, a
Wambundu-class medical ship called *Fleming* in the *Star Trek
Encyclopedia*. Eventually the reader might arrive at the Fleming
Davie meant – it was the travel writer Peter Fleming, Ian's elder
brother – but by then the sun would be rising over the chicken
coops. The bit about the ironmaster and Rider Haggard, I still
don't get. The trouble with giving any arcane reference an extra
twist of knowingness is that a reader halfway ignorant of your
meaning in the first place will be fully ignorant of it in the
second.

And yet, to borrow one of the poem's opening phrases, we sit
enthralled. Here is the proof that Davie had the magic, despite
his disguise as a resolutely lacklustre don. 'For showing Hector
was a mother's boy' has exactly the right density of obscurity.
Davie is brilliant on the way that history slides into the past, the

tumult of lived experience winking out to a set of slogans. 'An idiom too dated, Audenesque.' The line is itself dated and Audenesque, but it is a thrilling example of parody used as original material.

Davie, professedly content to forego all bardic privileges, could nevertheless show a startling lack of judgement in that regard, perhaps out of his misplaced admiration for the mind of Ezra Pound. We can blame Davie's humility for that: a proper measure of arrogance would have told him he could do things that Pound couldn't. For example, Pound couldn't write syntactically adroit and convincingly vocalised narrative quatrains. Davie had that gift by nature, but if he had pursued it further its demands might have disturbed him in his quiet solitude. Better to let the green adventure run to seed.

Japan

ANTHONY HECHT

1954

It was a miniature country once
To my imagination; Home of the Short,
And also the academy of stunts
    Where acrobats are taught
  The famous secrets of the trade:
  To cycle in the big parade
While spinning plates upon their parasols,
Or somersaults that do not touch the ground,
    Or tossing seven balls
In Most Celestial Order round and round.

A child's quick sense of the ingenious stamped
All their invention: toys I used to get
At Christmastime, or the peculiar, cramped
    Look of their alphabet.
  Fragile and easily destroyed,
  Those little boats of celluloid
Driven by camphor around the bathroom sink,
And delicate the folded paper prize
    Which, dropped into a drink
Of water, grew up right before your eyes.

Now when we reached them it was with a sense
Sharpened for treachery compounding in their brains

Like mating weasels; our Intelligence
     Said: The Black Dragon reigns
  Secretly under yellow skin,
     Deeper than dyes of atabrine
And deadlier. The War Department said:
Remember you are Americans; forsake
     The wounded and the dead
At your own cost; remember Pearl and Wake.

And yet they bowed us in with ceremony,
Told us what brands of Sake were the best,
Explained their agriculture in a phoney
     Dialect of the West,
  Meant vaguely to be understood
  As a shy sign of brotherhood
In the old human bondage to the facts
Of day-to-day existence. And like ants,
     Signalling tiny pacts
With their antennae, they would wave their hands.

At last we came to see them not as glib
Walkers of tightropes, worshipers of carp,
Nor yet a species out of Adam's rib
     Meant to preserve its warp
  In Cain's own image. They had learned
  That their tough eye-born goddess burned
Adoring fingers. They were very poor.
The holy mountain was not moved to speak.
     Wind at the paper door
Offered them snow out of its hollow peak.

Human endeavor clumsily betrays
Humanity. Their excrement served in this;
For, planting rice in water, they would raise
    Schistosomiasis
  Japonica, that enters through
  The pores into the avenue
And orbit of the blood, where it may foil
The heart and kill, or settle in the brain.
    This fruit of their nightsoil
Thrives in the skull, where it is called insane.

Now the quaint early image of Japan
That was so charming to me as a child
Seems like a bright design upon a fan,
    Of water rushing wild
  On rocks that can be folded up,
  A river which the wrist can stop
With a neat flip, revealing merely sticks
And silk of what had been a fan before,
    And like such winning tricks,
It shall be buried in excelsior.

━━◆━━

ANTHONY HECHT WAS WITH THE AMERICAN FORCES IN
Europe during the closing stages of the Second World War and
as might have been expected he wrote some important poems
about Nazi atrocities against Jews, but his most important poem
of the war was this one, written after the atomic bombs had

taken Japan out of military contention. On the face of it, the poem is scarcely about the war at all.

At one time in my life I spent several years studying the Japanese language and found that the mental effort required had a lot in common with trying to get toothpaste back into the tube. And the cost of taking your mind off the task, even for a month, is that you forget everything in a tearing hurry. The Japanese language is designed to be learned by children and used by adults. An adult learning it is asking for trouble. Hecht does a very good job of getting the essential tension into his poem: this is a culture that will always be out of reach.

When he, like thousands of other troops of the Occupation, arrived in Japan, they were told by their intelligence advisers that the Japanese were a tricky bunch. Hecht finds no signs of that. He loved the place, as all Westerners who spend any time there fall for Japan for the rest of their lives. This can be quite a shock, if you're convinced, as you should be, that the Japanese military effort was almost uniquely horrible.

If any other American could match Richard Wilbur's title as the Returned Second World War Poet with the whole caboodle in his kitbag, it was Hecht. He was a greatly gifted poet and this is a great poem: more than enough, with the suavely articulated turns and twists of its argument, to convince you that he had recovered from his traumatic exposure to the horrors of the Holocaust. But in fact what he saw at the liberation of Flossenbürg wrecked his sleep for years to come, so the serenity of this poem is all an illusion.

The American poetry guru, Helen Vendler, doesn't rate him. But then she scarcely rates Robert Frost either. (She did however spend a lot of time explaining why it was a big moment when

John Ashbery published a long poem on circular pages.) Hecht was distressed at her failure to mention him, but what he should have done was send her a written instruction to take a running jump at herself. Alas, he had a bump of reverence in the exact spot where he most needed a bump of arrogance.

In his student days he spent a lot of time hanging out with his future rivals for the limelight. Randall Jarrell, Allen Tate, Robert Penn Warren, John Crowe Ransom: the list, unfortunately, is endless. After the war he capped this propensity by seeing so much of Auden that nothing could allay the fascination except writing a book about him. Called *The Hidden Law*, it makes you wonder whether Hecht noticed that the chances of Auden's ever writing such a book in return were exactly zero.

If he had written the 'Japan' poem more recently, Hecht might have decided that excelsior, which mainly consisted of shredded paper and cardboard, was no longer the right term for packing material. But he would have needed to find a rhyme for styrofoam pellets.

A Baroque Wall-Fountain
in the Villa Sciarra

RICHARD WILBUR

1955

Under the bronze crown
Too big for the head of the stone cherub whose feet
    A serpent has begun to eat,
Sweet water brims a cockle and braids down

    Past spattered mosses, breaks
On the tipped edge of a second shell, and fills
    The massive third below. It spills
In threads then from the scalloped rim, and makes

    A scrim or summery tent
For a faun-ménage and their familiar goose.
    Happy in all that ragged, loose
Collapse of water, its effortless descent

    And flatteries of spray,
The stocky god upholds the shell with ease,
    Watching, about his shaggy knees,
The goatish innocence of his babes at play;

    His fauness all the while
Leans forward, slightly, into a clambering mesh
    Of water-lights, her sparkling flesh
In a saecular ecstasy, her blinded smile

Bent on the sand floor
Of the trefoil pool, where ripple-shadows come
    And go in swift reticulum,
More addling to the eye than wine, and more

    Interminable to thought
Than pleasure's calculus. Yet since this all
    Is pleasure, flash, and waterfall,
Must it not be too simple? Are we not

    More intricately expressed
In the plain fountains that Maderna set
    Before St. Peter's—the main jet
Struggling aloft until it seems at rest

    In the act of rising, until
The very wish of water is reversed,
    That heaviness borne up to burst
In a clear, high, cavorting head, to fill

    With blaze, and then in gauze
Delays, in a gnatlike shimmering, in a fine
    Illumined version of itself, decline,
And patter on the stones its own applause?

    If that is what men are
Or should be, if those water-saints display
    The pattern of our areté,
What of these showered fauns in their bizarre,

Spangled, and plunging house?
They are at rest in fulness of desire
   For what is given, they do not tire
Of the smart of the sun, the pleasant water-douse

    And riddled pool below,
Reproving our disgust and our ennui
   With humble insatiety.
Francis, perhaps, who lay in sister snow

    Before the wealthy gate
Freezing and praising, might have seen in this
   No trifle, but a shade of bliss—
That land of tolerable flowers, that state

    As near and far as grass
Where eyes become the sunlight, and the hand
   Is worthy of water: the dreamt land
Toward which all hungers leap, all pleasures pass.

———

IF WE COULD TURN BACK TIME, WE WOULD SEE RICHARD
Wilbur striding onstage in the American Embassy's auditorium
in London in the early 1960s. Imagine a mixture of the Great
Gatsby, Clark Gable, and Neil Armstrong getting set for walk-
ing into space, and you've got part of the picture. Imagine also
a candy-coloured jacket and the neat chinos of an Amherst Phi
Beta Kappa star student on vacation in Europe, and you've got
some of the rest of it. He was tall, handsome and dauntingly

cultivated. In the crowded auditorium male sighs competed with female sighs in a quiet storm of approbation and envy.

But the impression he made with the way he looked was a mere nothing compared to the impression he made when he spoke. And the poems he read were all his own, and it made you wonder why anyone else in the world was bothering to write anything. They were learned, packed with imagery, unfailingly lyrical. The first one to catch me by the heartstrings was this one, about the Baroque Wall-Fountain. One of Wilbur's great secrets was that every poem had at least something in it that would startle you on first reading, drawing you down into the poem's depths by the sheer dazzle of its surface flash. The whole of America's presence in the European War is in the poem's context, but the context keeps closing in on the narrator, until there is just him and the wall fountain, somewhere in Rome. Finally there is not even the fountain, but just the falling water.

Wilbur could do images so striking that you can only call them fabulous. There is a poem about Nijinsky in which the music 'flings / The dancer kneeling on nothing into the wings.' Try to get that image out of your head and you would break a chisel. Wilbur could write anything; he generated the critical lament that the typical bad American poem was the Wilbur poem not written by Wilbur. But there are no prizes for finding him predictable. In an early collection like *The Beautiful Changes*, one poem leads to another with such seeming inevitability only because his vision was unified, but what was it a vision of? It was the American world. Victorious America was taking over world culture, and indeed Wilbur's very presence in the American Embassy was part of America's assertion of itself in the face of what looked like the advance of Communism.

Wilbur was America's Yevgeny Yevtushenko with cool threads and a better haircut.

'The Baroque Wall-Fountain' is a war poem that makes you forget the war, as if there had never been any battles, though Wilbur had seen every battle from the Bulge onwards. In that battle, the Americans took ninety thousand casualties, yet Wilbur's tiny poem 'First Snow in Alsace' is the one that comes closest to capturing the scale of the disaster. Wilbur not only wrote some of the best post-war American poetry; he wrote some of the best post-war prose about poetry. His book *Responses* is a good demonstration of the advantage that the poet can sometimes enjoy over even the most accomplished critic. Poets know what they're talking about, even though they might be so dippy in real life that they can scarcely order lunch. Ultimately, in the long gaze of history, Wilbur was a testament to the GI Bill of Rights, the cranial hygiene conferred by the crewcut, and the paradoxical capacity of the American educational system to produce the occasional student who seems to have absorbed the culture of the entire universe.

On the Move

THOM GUNN
1957

The blue jay scuffling in the bushes follows
Some hidden purpose, and the gust of birds
That spurts across the field, the wheeling swallows,
Has nested in the trees and undergrowth.
Seeking their instinct, or their poise, or both,
One moves with an uncertain violence
Under the dust thrown by a baffled sense
Or the dull thunder of approximate words.

On motorcycles, up the road, they come:
Small, black, as flies hanging in heat, the Boys,
Until the distance throws them forth, their hum
Bulges to thunder held by calf and thigh.
In goggles, donned impersonality,
In gleaming jackets trophied with the dust,
They strap in doubt – by hiding it, robust –
And almost hear a meaning in their noise.

Exact conclusion of their hardiness
Has no shape yet, but from known whereabouts
They ride, direction where the tires press.
They scare a flight of birds across the field:
Much that is natural, to the will must yield.
Men manufacture both machine and soul,

And use what they imperfectly control
To dare a future from the taken routes.

It is a part solution, after all.
One is not necessarily discord
On earth; or damned because, half animal,
One lacks direct instinct, because one wakes
Afloat on movement that divides and breaks.
One joins the movement in a valueless world,
Choosing it, till, both hurler and the hurled,
One moves as well, always toward, toward.

A minute holds them, who have come to go:
The self-defined, astride the created will
They burst away; the towns they travel through
Are home for neither bird nor holiness,
For birds and saints complete their purposes.
At worst, one is in motion; and at best,
Reaching no absolute, in which to rest,
One is always nearer by not keeping still.

———

THOM GUNN WROTE SOME TREMENDOUS POEMS EARLY
on, and some poems almost equally tremendous in the last
phase of his life. Unfortunately there was a long stretch in the
middle – time spent mainly in America – where his poems
weren't tremendous at all. Here is a typical one called 'Listening
to Jefferson Airplane':

The music comes and goes in the wind,
Comes and goes on the brain.

And that was the whole poem. It didn't look very hard to do
when compared with some of his early and later work. But this
early poem 'On the Move', which is poetry in the great tradition
of lyrical argument, is a metaphysical disquisition dressed up as
an entertainment. It also has overtones of a Hell's Angels recruit-
ing poster, or a pamphlet published for the edification of early
members of the Waffen-SS.

Gunn loved the idea of roaring along on his motorbike like
Marlon Brando in *The Wild One*; and indeed it could be said
that in his static phase he lay around parts of California
achieving not much more than clouds of marijuana smoke
blown vertically. He got so peaceful back there that his
dreams of tough biker action became distant memories. What
once were paradigms of brutalist energy dissipated into fan-
tasy, as if the pace was being set not by roaring motorbikes
but by the members of 10CC who were merely dressing up as
motorcyclists.

At that point it is hard not to introduce our memories of the
figure cut by Yukio Mishima dressed only in motorbike boots
and a jockstrap, while leaning against his upright twin Honda.
Mishima ended up committing *seppuku*, and you might say that
Gunn did the same, but only at the artistic level. And it was on
the artistic level that he eventually came back, perhaps from
having realised that he had already used up his share of the
world's supply of high-quality grass.

In another famous early poem, Gunn said, 'I praise the over-
dogs from Alexander / To those who would not play with
Stephen Spender.' The slighting allusion was tough on Spender,

who gives us the impression of having been a dweeb only because he was so honest.

But on the whole Gunn's poems were full of movement, vigour and the confidence commensurate with his Sam-Shepard-standard handsomeness. One of the remarkable things about his career course was that his later poems returned to being almost as vivid pictorially as his first ones had been. Gunn early on perhaps took too much delight in dressing up as a stormtrooper on two wheels and dismissing the delicate aesthetes. Delicate aestheticism was one of his gifts, as we can see in the beginning of this poem, when he brings in the blue jay and the wheeling swallows. But the pastoral beginning is there only so that it can be shattered by the arrival of the bikers.

On the whole it is wise to avoid any poet who is capable of calling a volume *Fighting Terms* when he has never seen any real fighting, but on the other hand we should perhaps remember that Gunn lived his early life when to be an out gay male was still to be in hazard. And he had the courage of his art. In the middle of his life, when his artistic sense told him that nothing mattered except to drift around America looking vague and seeing vaguely, he had the courage to write small and trivial things. Then, later on, he returned to something like the full scale of his talent, which was a commanding one, to the extent that he should now be remembered as one of the majestic voices of his time. 'One is always nearer by not keeping still' is a reminder that poetry wouldn't matter at all if it didn't matter so much.

An Arundel Tomb

PHILIP LARKIN
1956

Side by side, their faces blurred,
The earl and countess lie in stone,
Their proper habits vaguely shown
As jointed armour, stiffened pleat,
And that faint hint of the absurd –
The little dogs under their feet.

Such plainness of the pre-baroque
Hardly involves the eye, until
It meets his left-hand gauntlet, still
Clasped empty in the other; and
One sees, with a sharp tender shock,
His hand withdrawn, holding her hand.

They would not think to lie so long.
Such faithfulness in effigy
Was just a detail friends would see:
A sculptor's sweet commissioned grace
Thrown off in helping to prolong
The Latin names around the base.

They would not guess how early in
Their supine stationary voyage
The air would change to soundless damage,
Turn the old tenantry away;

How soon succeeding eyes begin
To look, not read. Rigidly they

Persisted, linked, through lengths and breadths
Of time. Snow fell, undated. Light
Each summer thronged the glass. A bright
Litter of birdcalls strewed the same
Bone-riddled ground. And up the paths
The endless altered people came,

Washing at their identity.
Now, helpless in the hollow of
An unarmorial age, a trough
Of smoke in slow suspended skeins
Above their scrap of history,
Only an attitude remains:

Time has transfigured them into
Untruth. The stone fidelity
They hardly meant has come to be
Their final blazon, and to prove
Our almost-instinct almost true:
What will survive of us is love.

———

I THOUGHT THAT PHILIP LARKIN WAS SUCH A GREAT POET
that I wrote a whole book about him. Not a very big book, but
heartfelt. In my opinion he was the greatest English poet since
Marvell, with such a high standard that to choose a single poem

by him as representative is really an impossible task. Is the poem 'The Whitsun Weddings' really better than the poem 'Church Going'? No, they are in the most fruitful kind of contention, adding their complexities to each other in a process that we can confidently predict will never end.

There is too much ignorance in the world already to excuse any suggestion that a poem as beautiful as 'An Arundel Tomb' should be left undisturbed by any ancillary knowledge. We should always try to know more, and yet we should be careful that the facts don't leave us knowing less. The facts might say that the tomb was extensively restored during the nineteenth century, but what the poem says is that the figures on top of the tomb have always been there, looking the way they look now.

Larkin probably knew all there was to know about the tomb's history. It was a characteristic stratagem of his to feign ignorance about any subject that attracted his interest. 'Such plainness of the pre-baroque' powerfully suggests that he knows an awful lot about architecture for someone who is pretending not to. The figures on the tomb have drawn his attention on a level where he might have had little practical experience, but which he found consumingly interesting for that very reason. They were married, as he had never been.

Who were they? It tells you on the plinth. But the poet knows only or cares only that they are still together, travelling further into time even as he gazes upon 'their supine stationary voyage'. It's one of the great registrations in all his poetry of the difference between the personal and the eternal. The eternal is going on right there in front of you, but to contemplate it too long must reinforce the message that one day it will be going on without you. The tomb exemplifies everything that the poet has not got.

The story would be devastatingly sad if it were not for the way that the argument ends. Luckily it starts ending at the very beginning. The whole poem is a conclusion to itself. It would take a maniacal egotism to think that Larkin's account of the vanished quondam married couple is not a lament for the fate of all humanity. Occasionally some scholarly dolt, in a colossal feat of misplaced cleverness, manages to convince himself that the last line is about just 'us' – i.e. you and me – and not about all the people who ever lived, and ever will live. While to me it seems clear that the emphasis falls on the word 'survive' and not elsewhere, the dunce thinks that the emphasis is on 'us', as opposed to those two stone figures. (It's true that there is a recording of Larkin reading the poem that supports that emphasis, but I choose to ignore it. Poets are notoriously terrible at reading their own poems aloud.) Perhaps the dunce is distracted by that tempting word, 'almost', which suggests to him that Larkin was uncertain. But Larkin is exactly certain. One should hasten to say, though, that the poem can survive being misread or even being misread aloud, it's just so beautiful.

Last Meeting

GWEN HARWOOD
1957

Shadows grazing eastward melt
from their vast sun-driven flocks
into consubstantial dusk.
A snow wind flosses the bleak rocks,

strips from the gums their rags of bark,
and spins the coil of winter tight
round our last meeting as we walk
the littoral zone of day and night,

light's turncoat margin: rocks and trees
dissolve in nightfall-eddying waters;
tumbling whorls of cloud disclose
the cold eyes of the sea-god's daughters.

We tread the wrack of grass that once
a silver-bearded congregation
whispered about our foolish love.
Your voice in calm annunciation

from the dry eminence of thought
rings with astringent melancholy:
'Could hope recall, or wish prolong
the vanished violence of folly?

Minute by minute summer died;
time's horny skeletons have built
this reef on which our love lies wrecked.
Our hearts drown in their cardinal guilt.'

The world, said Ludwig Wittgenstein,
is everything that is the case.
 – The warmth of human lips and thighs;
the lifeless cold of outer space;

this windy darkness; Scorpio
above, a watercourse of light;
the piercing absence of one face
withdrawn for ever from my sight.

———————

I HAVE ALWAYS INTERPRETED THIS POEM AS A FAREWELL
to someone lost in the war. Reading it again in old age, I now
see there is no internal evidence in the poem that this is the case.
During the Second World War in Australia, most of the poets
saying goodbye were women. One of the more fruitful ironies
of the war was that this feminist poetic impetus never stopped.
Most deservedly prominent among the postwar women poets,
in my view, was Gwen Harwood. She had the invaluable gift of
musicality. 'Minute by minute summer died' shows she had the
technical wherewithal to be simple. 'The piercing absence of one
face / withdrawn for ever from my sight' is a final flourish on
the vibraharp that she makes sound easily and dreamily conclu-
sive, as if the jazz combo were signing off for half an hour to take

a few leisurely drinks. On the other hand, getting the whole of Ludwig Wittgenstein's name into an Australian poem was a feat comparable to Andrew Marvell's picking out all four syllables of 'magnanimous' in 'The Definition of Love'. One of the features of Harwood's poetry was this chain-lightning interchange between different levels of language. It takes a keen ear to do it successfully.

The way she specifies the lighting levels ('light's turncoat margin' tells us that the day is yielding to the night) proves that she was theatrical to the roots: though few poets were less bombastic, there were never that many who could give you such a hem-twirling sense that their latest poem was a real night out, with careful choice of accessories. When reading her aloud, it is advisable to remember that she was a performer, and would never have hurried the syllables so as to blur the stress pattern. A note in aid of recitation: it is hard to say 'littoral' and make it sound different from 'literal', but we should try.

At Seven O'Clock

1957

The masseur from Ceylon, whose balding head
Gives him a curious look of tenderness,
Uncurls his long crushed hands above my bed
As though he were about to preach or bless.

His poulterer's fingers pluck my queasy skin,
Shuffle along my side, and reach the thigh,
I note however that he keeps his thin
Fastidious nostrils safely turned away.

But sometimes the antarctic eyes glance down,
And the lids drop to hood a scornful flash:
A deep ironic knowledge of the thin
Or gross (but always ugly) human flesh.

Hernia, goitre and the flowering boil
Lie bare beneath his hands, for ever bare.
His fingers touch the skin: they reach the soul.
I know him in the morning for a seer.

Within my mind he is reborn as Christ:
For each blind dawn he kneads my prostrate thighs,
Thumps on my buttocks with his fist
And breathes, Arise.

———

WHEN I WAS LITERARY EDITOR OF THE SYDNEY UNIVERSITY student newspaper *honi soit* a copy of Oxford University's enviably glossy magazine *Isis* landed on my desk. It contained, as the latest instalment of its hagiographical series called 'Idol', a worshipping piece about Dom Moraes. Judging from his photograph he was only just out of his teens at the time. I was impressed by the generous welcome that the English seemed prepared to give Indians, and wondered vaguely if they might do the same for Australians. But what most impressed me was the way Moraes could write English verse.

'But sometimes the antarctic eyes glance down' unrolls with such rhythmic authority that it stops you wondering whether arctic eyes would be any different. I was impressed also by the way that 'flowering' managed to be the most disgusting word in a line-up of physical horrors. But the final stroke was the knockout punch. 'And breathes, Arise'. I went around saying it.

By the time I reached England, Moraes was well on his way to oblivion, having taken a swan dive into a bottle. Back he went to India, where he continued writing, but to small effect. It was a terrible pity, but finally nothing can stop the poets destroying themselves if they have a mind to. All other things being equal, theirs is the only life of perfect freedom. Quite often, however, that's exactly what scares them stupid.

John Marston Advises Anger

PETER PORTER

1961

All the boys are howling to take the girls to bed.
Our betters say it's a seedy world. The critics say
Think of them as an Elizabethan Chelsea set.
Then they've never listened to our lot – no talk
Could be less like – but the bodies are the same:
Those jeans and bums and sweaters of the King's Road
Would fit Marston's stage. What's in a name,
If Cheapside and the Marshalsea mean Eng. Lit.
And the Fantasie, Sa Tortuga, Grisbi, Bongi-Bo
Mean life? A cliché? What hurts dies on paper,
Fades to classic pain. Love goes as the MG goes.
The colonel's daughter in black stockings, hair
Like sash cords, face iced white, studies art,
Goes home once a month. She won't marry the men
She sleeps with, she'll revert to type – it's part
Of the side-show: Mummy and Daddy in the wings,
The bongos fading on the road to Haslemere
Where the inheritors are inheriting still.
Marston's Malheureux found his whore too dear;
Today some Jazz Club girl on the social make
Would put him through his paces, the aphrodisiac cruel.
His friends would be the smoothies of our Elizabethan age
The Rally Men, Grantchester Breakfast Men, Public School
Personal Assistants and the fragrant PROs,
Cavalry-twilled tame publishers praising Logue,

Classics Honours Men promoting Jazzetry,
Market Researchers married into Vogue.
It's a Condé Nast world and so Marston's was.
His had a real gibbet – our death's out of sight.
The same thin richness of these worlds remains –
The flesh-packed jeans, the car-stung appetite
Volley on his stage, the cage of discontent.

———

PETER PORTER COULD BE A DIFFICULT POET PRECISELY
because of his lack of a university education. Blessed with a
quick memory for almost all he read, he valued some of it too
much. One of the vital lessons that a university teaches by
surrounding you with learned people is that some of them will
be fools however much they know. Though there can be no
erudition without memory, there is no wisdom without judge-
ment. Judgement is the stuff you need to stop you writing a
poem about a Jacobean playwright whose short career was
fated to be looked back on fondly by almost nobody, although
T. S. Eliot, perhaps putting on a bit of dog, professed to find
him fascinating.

Porter's argument has a central premise: that Marston's stage,
'the cage of discontent', was a lot like London in the 1950s. And
so it perhaps was, except in every tangible respect. But it doesn't
matter, because of the yearning vividness with which Porter lists
the more recent tangible respects and revels in their depiction.
The 'flesh-packed jeans' and the 'car-stung appetite' take me back
to how the King's Road in Chelsea looked when I got off the boat

and stepped into the action, soon finding out that I couldn't afford to keep up with it.

Such, indeed, was the constant lament of Porter himself. 'Love goes as the MG goes'. The MG was an expensive little sports car and where it went was away, driven by someone else than you. The stunner draped in the passenger seat was beyond attainment. Actually she might not have been, but Porter was one of those charming men who talk themselves down, thus to avoid being distracted from their mission to complain about being alone.

Porter's hurtling gift for verse had the energy to offset the bitter ironies. He had the exuberance to make even his opacities glitter. Nobody remembers 'Jazzetry' now but you can guess it was a craze. Today, a long time later, there might be a few super-annuated sax players who remember noodling along in the background to some doomed poetry recital, but Porter would have faded along with the glossy scene he celebrated if he had not accepted that he was alone with his books and his classical-record collection. As things were, he made a joke out of being excluded from the glossy world and we all loved him for it, reciting his latest lines with thankful delight.

Poor Old Horse

DAVID HOLBROOK
1961

A child skipping jump on the quay at the Mill,
With parted legs jump, soft-footed in April,
   And the lovers on the bridge, sweet soft women's
      mouths
   Pressing jowls of men, in jeans or loose trousers, youths
   Packed in punts. And the masons on the bridge
   Pause as they lift white stone to dress the face of the ridge
   Of the balustrade, to imagine an actorish man
(Uxorious to a self-possessed blonde) as well as they can,
   Back in the hotel room, making love; they laugh,
   Turn back to the mortar. Ducks rise over trees, the chaff
   Of mixed men and women floats over. A boy with a
      shiny red face
Attentively wipes some beer from his sweetheart's sleeve.
      The place
I remember assignments of old at, by moon and water,
The same acts of living, the same weir-splashed
      happiness after.
But today I sit here alone – with my daughter rather,
Who critically watches the child skipping jump on the
      waterfall quay,
And we after go back to the car. I am dumb, and silent she.
   I see the spring love on the bridge for her: for me decay,
   Or at most the wry pretension, 'Well, we have had our
      day!'

I do not want to have had my day: I do not accept my
   jade,
Any more than the grey old horse we meet in the street,
His shaggy stiff dragged aside for a smart sports blade
And his smart sports car: yet that's no doubt my fate
As the water flows by here each year, April to April,
   With a soft-footed child skipping jump on the quay at the
   Mill.

———————

NOTHING COULD STOP DAVID HOLBROOK PRODUCING
books, unfortunately. In his role as a poet (he took every other
writing role as well) he would have been better had he slowed
down by a factor of about ten, but even as things were he still
managed to get the occasional thing written that made you
wonder whether the other chaps were really gaining all that
much by reining themselves in.

The above poem was in one of the early Penguin Modern
Poets collections and it knocked me out. Decades later it still
lifts my spirits, especially now that my once-tiny granddaughter
has become that very girl jumping soft-footed at the Mill. 'I do
not want to have had my day' is all the more powerful for being
placed as part of an argument with himself. He sounds very
alone.

Holbrook eventually wrote himself out of existence: he
was garrulous, which no poet can afford to be. Fluency is one
thing, but too much fluency is gush. It was an anomalous fate
for someone who went ashore on D-Day and had some very
real things to write about. Anyone who doubts Holbrook's

qualifications to write about them should look again at the picture of the little girl skipping jump on the quay at the Mill.

Lying in a Hammock at William Duffy's Farm in Pine Island, Minnesota

JAMES WRIGHT

1961

Over my head, I see the bronze butterfly
Asleep on the black trunk,
Blowing like a leaf in green shadow.
Down the ravine, behind the empty house,
The cowbells follow one another
Into the distances of the afternoon.
To my right,
In a field of sunlight between two pines,
The droppings of last year's horses
Blaze up like golden stones.
I lean back, as the evening darkens and comes on.
A chicken hawk floats over, looking for home.
I have wasted my life.

———

JAMES WRIGHT WAS THE AMERICAN WHO CONVINCED
aspiring poets all over the world that they could write poems
like this too. All they had to do, apparently, was pick a few
vignettes – how about that duck with the five ducklings trailing
behind it? – and make a point of leaving everything else out.
(Wait a second: the five ducklings are down to four.) How about
the dead cat that got run over by a truck? The question arises of

how we know it was a truck. Maybe it was a taxi. (And now the four ducklings are down to three.) Time to send a predatory bird flying overhead and quote some fancy Frenchman.

No, there is nothing to writing like this except the one crucial thing: you have to know what to leave out. And a second crucial thing: you need a sense of rhythm if you are going to fool with the rhythmically formless. The poem is out of tempo, but not arrhythmic, a nice tread for a poet to have, as it were. And a third crucial thing: he has a genial tone, a quality which can't be faked. The typical bad West Coast poem of the City Lights Bookstore era had a jokey tone, but no jokes.

At first I failed to notice that the last line of Wright's poem is lifted from Rimbaud: 'Par délicatesse / j'ai perdu ma vie.' But now I notice that the three ducklings are down to tw . . . wait a second. I've just realised that I'm writing a poem about a fox.

The Paper Nautilus

Marianne Moore
1961

For authorities whose hopes
are shaped by mercenaries?
   Writers entrapped by
   teatime fame and by
commuters' comforts? Not for these
   the paper nautilus
   constructs her thin glass shell.

   Giving her perishable
souvenir of hope, a dull
   white outside and smooth-
   edged inner surface
glossy as the sea, the watchful
   maker of it guards it
   day and night; she scarcely

   eats until the eggs are hatched.
Buried eight-fold in her eight
   arms, for she is in
   a sense a devil-
fish, her glass ram's-horn-cradled
   freight
   is hid but is not crushed;
   as Hercules, bitten

by a crab loyal to the hydra,
was hindered to succeed,
    the intensively
    watched eggs coming from
the shell free it when they are freed, –
    leaving its wasp-nest flaws
    of white on white, and close-

    laid Ionic chiton-folds
like the lines in the mane of
    a Parthenon horse,
    round which the arms had
wound themselves as if they knew love
    is the only fortress
    strong enough to trust to.

——————

For me, with regard to Marianne Moore, it's usually a case of the earlier the better. I have a very early pamphlet of her work printed by the Egoist Press, which I bought for almost nothing in Sydney when I was first a student and which I still treasure. (Quite possibly the Egoist Press's press for my pamphlet was hand-cranked by her fellow poet Ezra Pound.) In her later years, which started almost immediately, she got into a strange custom of altering poems from one edition to another, often to no detectable gain. Typically for her mature work, this poem 'Paper Nautilus' seems to have a line missing from its opening. This is almost certainly because there is a line missing. She got into bad habits of fiddling with perfection, and the bad habits verged on the tragic when you realised some of her ideas were indeed just that: perfect.

If Marianne Moore's chief drawback was that she couldn't stop altering her poems, her chief advantage was that she could see all the details of American life. Such were her powers of observation that it remains a pity she never wrote a poem about women factory workers constructing a B-29. During the Second World War women were working in the American aircraft factories, partly as a result of the equal status that had been exemplified for them by women like Eleanor Roosevelt and Marianne Moore. After the victory the renewed emphasis, in the world of advertising, on the well-dressed woman finding all of life's fulfilments in the kitchen was perceived as an attempt to return the place of women to the *status quo ante bellum*. In that context, Moore, from her tricorne hat downwards, looked as eccentric as a glide-on apparition from *Snow White and the Seven Dwarfs*; but her powers of sanity were piercing.

I didn't like the mad hatter aspect of Marianne Moore, partly because I didn't like the mad hat: tricornes are for pirates. And I couldn't and still can't stand syllabics: English is a rhythmic language and that's that. Or rather, that might not be entirely that, because the rhythm can vary, but spotting the rhythm should be a requirement always, and counting the syllables never. But I forgive Marianne Moore because her ideas carried such a wealth of specific suggestion. The nautilus's 'wasp-nest flaws / of white on white' are no sooner said than seen. She is perfectly right, having seen a morphological similarity between species that really have no relation to each other until a great poet comes along and perceives the echo. 'close- / laid Ionic chiton-folds' precisely evoke the statue of a Greek soldier in his fighting tunic. A quotation like 'the lines in the mane of / a

Parthenon horse' could be the start of another poem, but only a poem by her. All of the images mentioned in the previous sentences occur within the same few lines. So much material packed in such a small space would ordinarily make for an effect of density, which is to say, of heavy immobility, but she doesn't just observe; she comments, and quite often the comment takes you somewhere else. The whole effect is of lightness and delicacy.

Incidentally, when she read one of her syllabic poems aloud, she couldn't help putting the rhythm back in – the sure sign of the born poet, along with faultless eyesight.

Cut

SYLVIA PLATH
1962

What a thrill—
My thumb instead of an onion.
The top quite gone
Except for a sort of hinge

Of skin,
A flap like a hat,
Dead white.
Then that red plush.

Little pilgrim,
The Indian's axed your scalp.
Your turkey wattle
Carpet rolls

Straight from the heart.
I step on it,
Clutching my bottle
Of pink fizz.

A celebration, this is.
Out of a gap
A million soldiers run,
Redcoats, every one.

Whose side are they on?
O my
Homunculus, I am ill.
I have taken a pill to kill

The thin
Papery feeling.
Saboteur,
Kamikaze man—

The stain on your
Gauze Ku Klux Klan
Babushka
Darkens and tarnishes and when

The balled
Pulp of your heart
Confronts its small
Mill of silence

How you jump—
Trepanned veteran,
Dirty girl,
Thumb stump.

———◆———

THIS SYLVIA PLATH POEM SHOULD REALLY BE CALLED
'Kamikaze Man' instead of just 'Cut'. If you can evoke a Japanese
aircraft screaming in a death-dive, why confine your imagery to

the humble realm of the kitchen? Sylvia Plath's kitchen might have shown touches of American expectations, but basically she was stuck in poverty-stricken post-war England, along with her famous but not yet affluent husband, Ted Hughes.

I read this poem the month it was published in *London* magazine, during the bad winter of 1962, and I thought: if she can do this, she can do anything. Not even Hughes ever pulled off a thing like 'Cut' – his poem 'Pike' was good, but basically it was the story of a fight between a tiny fish and a huge man, whereas Plath's poem had a world war in it. She continued to think on a world scale while Hughes occupied himself with voles and weasels. Or perhaps I mean weevils. The paradox presented by the couple was that Plath was the giant. Although the towering Hughes raided the whole of history and all cultures for his ideas, she was the one with the poetic scope. If her suicide was a self-criticism, it was a terrible error.

For one thing, it deprived us of her sense of rhythm, which was as rich and varied as a well-stocked jukebox. She could make her verses swing beautifully, like the swish of a well-cut skirt. Immediately, one thinks of a co-ed bopping smoothly around a college room. Though she had the kind of background and upbringing that made her a target for *Vogue* advertisements – when she wrote for *Vogue* it was a natural fit – she retained the dewy innocence of the teenager. There was something of the cheerleader about her even under her fundamental seriousness that makes her tragedy all the more hard to bear.

She could write like this, and yet she killed herself. Where did the angst come from? No wonder so many people, and especially so many feminists, blamed Hughes for her demise. It was easier than blaming fate. But in fact, as this little poem about a mere cut thumb suggests, she had a sense of disaster built in. Who taught her that there might be a connection between a bloody bandage and a 'dirty girl'? Perhaps she had a sense of life that was worried by death all along, and sought it out in order to finish solving a mystery.

Sandpiper

ELIZABETH BISHOP
1962

The roaring alongside he takes for granted,
and that every so often the world is bound to shake.
He runs, he runs to the south, finical, awkward,
in a state of controlled panic, a student of Blake.

The beach hisses like fat. On his left, a sheet
of interrupting water comes and goes
and glazes over his dark and brittle feet.
He runs, he runs straight through it, watching his toes.

— Watching, rather, the spaces of sand between them
where (no detail too small) the Atlantic drains
rapidly backwards and downwards. As he runs,
he stares at the dragging grains.

The world is a mist. And then the world is
minute and vast and clear. The tide
is higher or lower. He couldn't tell you which.
His beak is focussed; he is preoccupied,

looking for something, something, something.
Poor bird, he is obsessed!
The millions of grains are black, white, tan, and gray
mixed with quartz grains, rose and amethyst.

Elizabeth Bishop observed nature so well that her only danger lay in observing it too long and too finely. Her famous poem 'The Fish' is almost fatally damaged by the fact that the description goes on so long before she gives up and throws the fish back in: it would have started to decay by then.

In the poem about the sandpiper hopping along the beach, the bird's mentality is so sharply evoked (it hears the hissing water) that you can't help wondering about its taste for Blake. Where does it keep its library? At the back of the nest, perhaps. Apart from the Blake moment, the whole poem is quite believably written in avian terms, with the cumulative effect that the protagonist of this little drama is clearly not human. Bishop has transported her vast capacity for perception into a birdbrain. The sandpiper is out there on the beach, looking at it through its eyes instead of ours, but seeing everything as if its eyes are wired up to a large intelligence. The conceit works. In fact, the conceit is the poem's hero. It is really a poem about how a poem is about something.

Always the thoughtful anchor of any house she lived in, Bishop had the capacity to analyse experience all the way to its roots in evolutionary psychology. She once told her great friend and mentor Robert Lowell that it was hopelessly bad manners to use his ex-wife Elizabeth Hardwick's personal letters to him unchanged as poetic material. Lowell ignored her. In other chapters of his episodic mental life he cultivated a well-deserved reputation for insanity. (On some of his later transatlantic flights he would propose marriage to the air hostess, often an awkward moment in view of the fact that he was already married to someone else.) Despite her own aberrations – she was a drinker on an epic scale – Bishop was a model of sanity. She was morally a towering genius compared to Lowell, but then so am I, and so was Scrooge McDuck.

Though she was continually expiring from nerves and took ages to complete anything, the best of her finished poems make her look like a model of creative confidence. Her later life was a triumph of artistic integrity over inner turmoil. It's worth remembering that it takes either a liberal democracy or a rich benefactor and preferably both to keep an artist like her in business. In Bishop's case, one of the benefactors was the poet James Merrill, who was slightly less rich each time that he realised she could use some financial support. She did, however, use it. The quality of her work shines brighter all the time.

Dream Song 4

JOHN BERRYMAN
1964? 1968?

Filling her compact & delicious body
with chicken páprika, she glanced at me
twice.
Fainting with interest, I hungered back
and only the fact of her husband & four other people
kept me from springing on her

or falling at her little feet and crying
'You are the hottest one for years of night
Henry's dazed eyes
have enjoyed, Brilliance.' I advanced upon
(despairing) my spumoni. —Sir Bones: is stuffed,
de world, wif feeding girls.

—Black hair, complexion Latin, jewelled eyes
downcast . . . The slob beside her feasts . . . What
    wonders is
she sitting on, over there?
The restaurant buzzes. She might as well be on Mars.
Where did it all go wrong? There ought to be a law
    against Henry.
— Mr. Bones: there is.

OF ALL OF JOHN BERRYMAN'S 'DREAM SONGS', THIS ONE is the most outrageous. So why choose it? Well, it is also the most alive with his vaudevillian magic, so the offended reader will have to put up with its knowingly transgressive tone, or else miss the deeper impulse of Berryman's poetry. The deeper impulse is sex. In his personae as the narrator and the narrator's outrageous companion, Mr Bones (think of them as the First and Second Banana, and get ready for the loud, lewd snap of the slap-stick), Berryman and his alter ego rush on stage in lock-step and jointly tear up the joint. 'What wonders is / she sitting on, over there?' It only sounds like a rude question. It is, in fact, a very rude question.

Alas, a lot of Berryman's energy was tied to his rampant libido. But in that respect he had at least one predecessor of great gifts: Rochester. (Along, of course, with all those predecessors without much of a gift at all.) Beside Rochester, Berryman merely flirts with dirt. But the question remains open of whether pornography and poetry are compatible at all.

Pornography and prose, yes: back in the eighteenth century, John Cleland's *Fanny Hill* put quite a lot of linguistic elegance in amongst the rumpy-pumpy, and in recent times Terry Southern was always more gifted than the genre demanded. But Apollinaire's career tips us off to the proper order of events. His prose was the vehicle for his mere scurrilities and his poetry the home for his true talents.

Will Not Come Back

1969

Dark swallows will doubtless come back killing
the injudicious nightflies with a clack of the beak;
but these that stopped full flight to see your beauty
and my good fortune . . . as if they knew our
    names—
they'll not come back. The thick lemony honey-
    suckle,
climbing from earthroot to your window,
will open more beautiful blossoms to the evening;
but these . . . like dewdrops, trembling, shining,
    falling,
the tears of day—they'll not come back . . .
Some other love will sound his fireword for you
and wake your heart, perhaps, from its cool sleep;
but silent, absorbed, and on his knees,
as men adore God at the altar, as I love you—
don't blind yourself, you'll not be loved like that.

———

THE ABOVE POEM IS A VERSION, OR A TRANSLATION: A
word which usually means, with Robert Lowell, that the original
is only dimly in sight and typically unacknowledged. Here the
plundered victim is the nineteenth-century Spanish poet G. A.

258

Bécquer. Nevertheless, it's a poem great enough to justify the theft.

'But these that stopped full flight to see your beauty . . .' Stopping in full flight is quite a hard thing for swallows to pull off even when love-struck, but poetry is a magic land – or perhaps it's better to call it a mad land. During various episodes in his life, Lowell was as mad as a hatter, but in poems like these he went crazy for a purpose. He could make a surrealist landscape feel like a real one.

Prodigiously gifted and ambitious, Lowell was a long time working his way to this kind of simplicity, and then later on he lost it again. Back in his early collections, a poem like 'The Quaker Graveyard in Nantucket' was as gnarled and twisted as a sea-blown tree. With his intermediate volume *Life Studies*, he became famous for his 'confessional verse' which too often consisted of confessing the embarrassments of other people. It was his worst habit.

As the bird with the air-brakes demonstrates, Lowell could rise to sublimity and fall to banality within a single phrase. The key poem of his full maturity was 'For the Union Dead' where his twin-yoked capacities for complexity and simplicity worked sumptuously together. In his later and last phase, he was using his own early poems as raw material: the whole of *Notebook* consists of his early poems cut to the lengths of sonnets, sometimes with the effect of a madman scissoring off the end of a sock in order to give his toes more freedom.

For all of us on the Soho literary scene, Lowell featured like a visiting brontosaurus. I can remember well one of his editors cowering behind his desk at the prospect of his American-aristocrat-star-contributor suddenly appearing with a fresh crate of sonnets. But this poem and a few others show unmistakably the precision, compression and evocation of which he was capable when sane. A sharp reminder, there, that insanity is always a great pity, and a double reminder that it rarely leads to definitive creativity. But let's not forget the third reminder: that talent has a mind of its own, and sometimes prevails against all the inner turmoil that can threaten to wreck a life.

Pike

TED HUGHES
1969

Pike, three inches long, perfect
Pike in all parts, green tigering the gold.
Killers from the egg: the malevolent aged grin.
They dance on the surface among the flies.

Or move, stunned by their own grandeur,
Over a bed of emerald, silhouette
Of submarine delicacy and horror.
A hundred feet long in their world.

In ponds, under the heat-struck lily pads –
Gloom of their stillness:
Logged on last year's black leaves, watching upwards.
Or hung in an amber cavern of weeds

The jaws' hooked clamp and fangs
Not to be changed at this date:
A life subdued to its instrument;
The gills kneading quietly, and the pectorals.

Three we kept behind glass,
Jungled in weed: three inches, four,
And four and a half: fed fry to them –
Suddenly there were two. Finally one

With a sag belly and the grin it was born with.
And indeed they spare nobody.
Two, six pounds each, over two feet long
High and dry and dead in the willow-herb –

One jammed past its gills down the other's gullet:
The outside eye stared: as a vice locks –
The same iron in this eye
Though its film shrank in death.

A pond I fished, fifty yards across,
Whose lilies and muscular tench
Had outlasted every visible stone
Of the monastery that planted them –

Stilled legendary depth:
It was as deep as England. It held
Pike too immense to stir, so immense and old
That past nightfall I dared not cast

But silently cast and fished
With the hair frozen on my head
For what might move, for what eye might move.
The still splashes on the dark pond,

Owls hushing the floating woods
Frail on my ear against the dream
Darkness beneath night's darkness had freed,
That rose slowly toward me, watching.

Ted Hughes should have been more at home out on the river in waders murdering fish than sitting down at a desk composing poetry about them. But the truth was that behind the desk was where he truly belonged. We might guess, when we read his famous early poem about the jaguar, that he had spent time in exotic jungles, but in fact he had spent time at the zoo. 'Over the cage floor the horizons come': I still find myself saying that, even as the last horizon approaches like a – well, like a jaguar, really. He wrote that line a long time ago but it got into my head and it's still there.

In his poem about 'The Pike', when you encounter the tiny pike's 'malevolent aged grin' you know straightaway that you are in the presence of transformative poetry. 'Amber cavern of weeds' is also magic, a Merlin-type magic. No wonder Sylvia Plath went for him. Indeed, she bit a piece out of him at their first meeting. It might have been better for both of them if this small act of cannibalism had signalled the end of their relationship rather than its beginning, but the die was cast. That last phrase comes from Suetonius about Julius Caesar, and was also used by Shakespeare in *Richard III*, a fact of which Hughes would have been well aware, because he was saturated in Shakespeare, to the point of conceiving superfluous theoretical treatises on the subject.

Unfortunately, Hughes was also marinated in mysticism. He could gush at enormous length on cabalistic matters: voodoo and necromancy became far too natural for a man whose business should have been clarity. There were clouds of smoke, stirred only by the beat of tom-toms. Meaningfulness flooded in as meaning fled.

Supposedly his famous poetic hero The Thought-Fox was

based on a creature he saw one night in the front court of Pembroke College, but it might have been another undergraduate. Hughes was so tall that any other student looked low-slung to him. The last time I saw him was at Buckingham Palace, where he looked as if he owned the joint. He paid me such a compliment ('I've been watching your comet crossing the sky') that I had no choice but to fall in love with him. He was one of the most handsome men I've ever seen.

Shore Woman

SEAMUS HEANEY
C. 1969

> Man to the hills, woman to the shore.
> *Gaelic proverb*

I have crossed the dunes with their whistling bent
Where dry loose sand was riddling round the air
And I'm walking the firm margin. White pocks
Of cockle, blanched roofs of clam and oyster
Hoard the moonlight, woven and unwoven
Off the bay. At the far rocks
A pale sud comes and goes.

Under boards the mackerel slapped to death
Yet still we took them in at every cast,
Stiff flails of cold convulsed with their first breath.
My line plumbed certainly the undertow,
Loaded against me once I went to draw
And flashed and fattened up towards the light.
He was all business in the stern. I called
'This is so easy that it's hardly right,'
But he unhooked and coped with frantic fish
Without speaking. Then suddenly it lulled,
We'd crossed where they were running, the line
    rose
Like a let-down and I was conscious
How far we'd drifted out beyond the head.

'Count them up at your end', was all he said
Before I saw the porpoises' thick backs
Cartwheeling like the flywheels of the tide,
Soapy and shining. To have seen a hill
Splitting the water could not have numbed me
    more
Than the close irruption of that school,
Tight viscous muscle, hooped from tail to snout,
Each one revealed complete as it bowled out
And under.
                    They will attack a boat.
I knew it and I asked him to put in
But he would not, declared it was a yarn
My people had been fooled by far too long
And he would prove it now and settle it.
Maybe he shrank when those sloped oily backs
Propelled towards us: I lay and screamed
Under splashed brine in an open rocking boat
Feeling each dunt and slither through the timber,
Sick at their huge pleasures in the water.

I sometimes walk this strand for thanksgiving
Or maybe it's to get away from him
Skittering his spit across the stove. Here
Is the taste of safety, the shelving sand
Harbours no worse than razor-shell or crab
Though my father recalls carcasses of whales
Collapsed and gasping, right up to the dunes.
But tonight such moving sinewed dreams lie out
In darker fathoms, far beyond the head.
Astray upon a debris of scrubbed shells

Between parched dunes and salivating wave,
I have rights on this fallow avenue,
A membrane between moonlight and my shadow.

———

DESPITE THE ALMOST DELIBERATE-SOUNDING SELF-parody in one or two of its introductory phrases ('white pocks / Of cockle' sounds so like him it verges on spoof status), this was the poem that convinced me that Seamus Heaney was beyond good. All the bits about the mackerel and the cod counted as perceptions but the porpoises, 'cartwheeling like the flywheels of the tide', counted as a vision. The only possible answer to the question 'How did he think of that?' was 'Because he's him.' Purists might point out that the metaphor is a mixed one but they will hardly distract us from our entranced astonishment.

As a poet who never severed his ties to Ireland, Heaney had a political tightrope to walk. We are lucky he did not get shot at from two different directions. Nevertheless he won through to attain a venerable senior status. I was present at one of his latter-day readings in London and I wondered if there had ever been quite so charming a poetic voice. Dylan Thomas could cast thrilling spells but this man could climb the heights of expressiveness just by taking it easy: by chaise-longue to Everest.

Modesty demands that I should not be strident in asserting my claim that I was first to call him Seamus Feamus. Historical veracity, on the other hand, insists that I assert my proprietary rights to the term. That's what I called him, in my 1974 mock-epic *Peregrine Prykke's Pilgrimage*, which will probably not be back in print again before Hell freezes over. No mystery, then, as to why I should not want its moments of truth to be forgotten. Seamus Feamus was the exact thing to call him. He was born for glory: you could tell that before he spoke, and when he spoke he made hundreds of years of troubled history seem at least a touch more bearable.

Sea Grapes

Derek Walcott
1976

That sail which leans on light,
tired of islands,
a schooner beating up the Caribbean

for home, could be Odysseus,
home-bound on the Aegean;
that father and husband's

longing, under gnarled sour grapes, is
like the adulterer hearing Nausicaa's name
in every gull's outcry.

This brings nobody peace. The ancient war
between obsession and responsibility
will never finish and has been the same

for the sea-wanderer or the one on shore
now wriggling on his sandals to walk
    home,
since Troy sighed its last flame,

and the blind giant's boulder heaved the
    trough
from whose groundswell the great
    hexameters come

to the conclusions of exhausted surf.

The classics can console. But not enough.

———

DEREK WALCOTT HAD MORE TALENT THAN ANYONE KNEW what to do with. He was the most successful pupil in the St Kitts school system but he missed out on his scholarship to England, and therefore had to stay in the Caribbean. It was a stroke of luck both for him and for us. He grew to maturity in surroundings even richer than his gift. To be that, they had to be lush and abundant. His poems teem with places you would like to be, fish you would like to chase, fruit you would like to eat, and a sensitivity to these things that you would like to have. It's no wonder that so many of his poems were big: he had a lot of stuff he felt compelled to fit into them.

This short poem, however, gives you the lightning strike of his talent without taking an hour out of your life. His use of the Homeric properties is brilliantly inventive. Every poet from the big civilisations wrote, has written or is still writing poems with Nausicaa in them, but Walcott noticed and remembered that the name really does sound like a gull's cry. The idea that the rocks thrown from his volcanic crater by the angry Cyclops caused ripples that were pre-echoes of the poetic hexameter is beyond clever. It's poetic.

Most of Walcott's short poems go on for ten pages at least, so he didn't get much practice with the kind of closing line that unmistakably shuts the poem down, but this time he got it perfectly right. If you look again at the last line of Robert Lowell's

'The Quaker Graveyard in Nantucket' ('The Lord survives the rainbow of His will'), you find a puzzle. Walcott's closing line gives a cleaner ending. For a compulsive writer of epics and semi-epics, the poem thus becomes, and becomes decisively, a rare example of successful brevity.

Not My Best Side

U.A. FANTHORPE
1978

I

Not my best side, I'm afraid.
The artist didn't give me a chance to
Pose properly, and as you can see,
Poor chap, he had this obsession with
Triangles, so he left off two of my
Feet. I didn't comment at the time
(What, after all, are two feet
To a monster?) but afterwards
I was sorry for the bad publicity.
Why, I said to myself, should my conqueror
Be so ostentatiously beardless, and ride
A horse with a deformed neck and square hoofs?
Why should my victim be so
Unattractive as to be inedible,
And why should she have me literally
On a string? I don't mind dying
Ritually, since I always rise again,
But I should have liked a little more blood
To show they were taking me seriously.

II

It's hard for a girl to be sure if
She wants to be rescued. I mean, I quite
Took to the dragon. It's nice to be

Liked, if you know what I mean. He was
So nicely physical, with his claws
And lovely green skin, and that sexy tail,
And the way he looked at me,
He made me feel he was all ready to
Eat me. And any girl enjoys that.
So when this boy turned up, wearing machinery,
On a really dangerous horse, to be honest
I didn't much fancy him. I mean,
What was he like underneath the hardware?
He might have acne, blackheads or even
Bad breath for all I could tell, but the dragon –
Well, you could see all his equipment
At a glance. Still, what could I do?
The dragon got himself beaten by the boy,
And a girl's got to think of her future.

III

I have diplomas in Dragon
Management and Virgin Reclamation.
My horse is the latest model, with
Automatic transmission and built-in
Obsolescence. My spear is custom-built,
And my prototype armour
Still on the secret list. You can't
Do better than me at the moment.
I'm qualified and equipped to the
Eyebrow. So why be difficult?
Don't you want to be killed and / or rescued
In the most contemporary way? Don't
You want to carry out the roles

That sociology and myth have designed for you?
Don't you realise that, by being choosy,
You are endangering job prospects
In the spear- and horse-building industries?
What, in any case, does it matter what
You want? You're in my way.

———

You don't have to have seen the Paolo Uccello painting of St George and the Dragon in London's National Gallery to appreciate U.A. Fanthorpe's sumptuously panoramic poem, but it helps if you know the layout. In the pre-modern manner, the whole story takes place in the one frame of the painting, with the dragon at the centre, St George arriving on horseback at the right, and our threatened girl on the left. The dragon and the knight get a speech each, but the star speaker is the princess, rather unfairly described as less than riveting. But when she talks, she seems enchanted, and less so by St George than by the dragon.

The device of her talking works brilliantly, mainly because Fanthorpe has a sensitivity to the tones of officialese that brings out the pomposity of the formulaic. Kingsley Amis always advised against writing a poem about a painting, but this poem alone is enough to demonstrate that he was wrong.

Still almost totally unknown, Fanthorpe was once a candidate for Oxford Professor of Poetry, but the electorate wasn't ready for a woman. It was the nearest she ever got to being famous. (She got a taste of fame when Carol Ann Duffy, on the verge of the laureateship, saluted her as the necessary predecessor.) On the strength of this poem alone, she should have been hailed as one of the great British poets of modern times.

Dragon Management, Virgin Reclamation – the quiet wit of Fanthorpe depends on reading and listening. A poet should be always on the alert for what is happening in the common language. If I was young and strong again I would learn this one, and as things are I have most of it by heart anyway. It has all the prose virtues as well as the poetic ones. None of the witty male poets were quite as witty as she is in catching the more pompous turns of official and critical language, and turning them to comic use: 'endangering job prospects / In the spear- and horse-building industries.' In that regard, she was as clever as Wendy Cope.

In this poem Fanthorpe has worked the essential trick of the witty poet, by making the reader feel witty too. The whole poem fairly crackles with the kind of linguistic knowingness that Philip Larkin and Kingsley Amis got famous for. But not even they managed something quite so subversive. In their poems about desire, men often fancied women, women sometimes fancied men, but no women at all fancied dragons. The scenario is outrageous: a quality emphasised by its delicacy of language. 'It's nice to be / Liked' is the tone of a girl. The childish voice means that she's submitting, a little girl being led astray by a giant male stranger. A fantastic achievement, that stanza, in which the girl childishly gives way to her fate as the dragon's plaything, or perhaps his lunch.

It's notable that Uccello combined his masterly sinuosity – check out the riverine fall of the girl's gown – with a complete control of perspective, which really depends on very straight lines vanishing into the distance. See the way the pieces of broken lance in his painting about the battle of San Romano are lined up and vanish into the distance along the orthogonals. There's a mathematical precision either under or beside or – more likely – commingling with his gift for the sinuous.

In the first year that I was courting my future wife in Florence, she, already an expert on the Renaissance, took me to see Uccello's Green Cloister fresco in Santa Maria Novella. I was knocked out, especially by the tall lady on the left, and promised us both that we would come back tomorrow to see it all properly. Next morning a sign appeared saying that the fresco was now *in restauro* – being restored. And indeed it was, for the next fifteen years. There was a lesson there somewhere; get the first appreciation done at the time.

Mrs Midas

CAROL ANN DUFFY

1999

It was late September. I'd just poured a glass of
   wine, begun
to unwind, while the vegetables cooked. The kitchen
filled with the smell of itself, relaxed, its steamy breath
gently blanching the windows. So I opened one,
then with my fingers wiped the other's glass like a brow.
He was standing under the pear tree snapping a twig.

Now the garden was long and the visibility poor, the way
the dark of the ground seems to drink the light of the sky,
but that twig in his hand was gold. And then he plucked
a pear from a branch – we grew Fondante
   d'Automne –
and it sat in his palm, like a lightbulb. On.
I thought to myself, Is he putting fairy lights in the tree?

He came into the house. The doorknobs gleamed.
He drew the blinds. You know the mind; I thought of
the Field of the Cloth of Gold and of Miss Macready.
He sat in that chair like a king on a burnished throne.
The look on his face was strange, wild, vain. I said,
What in the name of God is going on? He started to laugh.

I served up the meal. For starters, corn on the cob.
Within seconds he was spitting out the teeth of the rich.

He toyed with his spoon, then mine, then with
　　the knives, the forks.
He asked where was the wine. I poured with a shaking hand,
a fragrant, bone-dry white from Italy, then watched
as he picked up the glass, goblet, golden chalice, drank.

It was then that I started to scream. He sank to his knees.
After we'd both calmed down, I finished the wine
on my own, hearing him out. I made him sit
on the other side of the room and keep his hands to himself.
I locked the cat in the cellar. I moved the phone.
The toilet I didn't mind. I couldn't believe my ears:

how he'd had a wish. Look, we all have wishes; granted.
But who has wishes granted? Him. Do you know about gold?
It feeds no one; aurum, soft, untarnishable; slakes
no thirst. He tried to light a cigarette; I gazed, entranced,
as the blue flame played on its luteous stem. At least,
I said, you'll be able to give up smoking for good.

Separate beds. In fact, I put a chair against my door,
near petrified. He was below, turning the spare room
into the tomb of Tutankhamun. You see, we were
　　passionate then,
in those halcyon days; unwrapping each other, rapidly,
like presents, fast food. But now I feared his
　　honeyed embrace,
the kiss that would turn my lips to a work of art.

And who, when it comes to the crunch, can live
with a heart of gold? That night, I dreamt I bore

278

his child, its perfect ore limbs, its little tongue
like a precious latch, its amber eyes
holding their pupils like flies. My dream milk
burned in my breasts. I woke to the streaming sun.

So he had to move out. We'd a caravan
in the wilds, in a glade of its own. I drove him up
under the cover of dark. He sat in the back.
And then I came home, the woman who married the fool
who wished for gold. At first, I visited, odd times,
parking the car a good way off, then walking.

You knew you were getting close. Golden trout
on the grass. One day, a hare hung from a larch,
a beautiful lemon mistake. And then his footprints,
glistening next to the river's path. He was thin,
delirious; hearing, he said, the music of Pan
from the woods. Listen. That was the last straw.

What gets me now is not the idiocy or greed
but lack of thought for me. Pure selfishness. I sold
the contents of the house and came down here.
I think of him in certain lights, dawn, late afternoon,
and once a bowl of apples stopped me dead. I miss most,
even now, his hands, his warm hands on my skin, his touch.

IT NEVER HURTS A POEM TO HAVE A MOMENT THAT MAKES the reader fall out of his chair, as long as the poem goes on being interesting to the end. Amy Clampitt's poem about the cheetah sins in this regard: nothing else in the poem beats the picture of the floral markings on the animal's coat changing to a sandstorm when the creature runs. But Carol Ann Duffy has devised a sufficiently brilliant setting for the teeth of King Midas, and incidentally written one of the perfect poems of the late twentieth century. Her laureateship, one feels, was the least she had coming. Just think of those corny teeth rattling into the plate and you've got the essence of poetic imagery in a flash: it's the sound of a picture.

The gold teeth on the cob is merely likely to be the image that hits you first. Go back through the poem and you'll find there's something astonishing happening every couple of lines. Appropriately, the poem is a whole treasure house: the teeth of the rich; the pear that sits in his hand like a light bulb; the kiss that would turn her lips to a work of art; 'its little tongue / like a precious latch'; 'and who, when it comes to the crunch, can live / with a heart of gold?' And so it goes on, hit moment after hit moment; until finally you see that the whole thing adds up to a picture of terrible loneliness. The most certain way of being cast out of heaven is to be cursed with a supernatural advantage. Or to put it another way, heaven and hell are only a subway-stop apart. But now she's got me doing it. If only I could do it as well as she.

Basho in Ireland

BILLY COLLINS
2016

I am like the Japanese poet
who longed to be in Kyoto
even though he was already in Kyoto.

I am not exactly like him
because I am not Japanese
and I have no idea what Kyoto is like

But once, while walking around
the Irish town of Ballyvaughan
I caught myself longing to be in Ballyvaughan.

The sense of being homesick
for a place that is not my home
while being right in the middle of it

was particularly strong
when I passed the hotel bar
then the fluorescent depth of a laundrette,

also when I stood at the crossroads
with the road signs pointing in 3 directions
and the enormous buses making the turn.

It might have had something to do
with the nearby limestone hills
and the rain collecting on my collar,

but then again I have longed
to be with a number of people
while the two of us were sitting in a room

on an ordinary evening
without a limestone hill in sight,
thousands of miles from Kyoto

and the simple wonders of Ballyvaughan,
which reminds me
of another Japanese poet

who wrote how much he enjoyed
not being able to see
his favourite mountain because of all the fog.

———

In this deceptively modest poem, Billy Collins,
who not long ago was America's Poet Laureate, deploys faux-
naive as a mode, with just a little dash of wasabi.

Basho was the seventeenth-century Japanese poet who took,
in his resonant phrase, the narrow road to the deep north. His
journey became world-famous, to the extent that people today
recognise his name as that of a Japanese poet even when they
know nothing about Japanese poetry. I might sound a bit

repetitively simple when saying all this, but perhaps I've been infected by Collins's tone, which pulls off the difficult trick of letting you know that it is *meant* to be faux-naive.

Early in the poem the trick perhaps falters, when he claims not to know what Kyoto is like. Five strokes on the computer keyboard would give him pages of information about what Kyoto is like. (We have entered the age in which, in relation to anything at all, total ignorance is impossible; which makes feigning it a lost cause.)

I have actually sat on a wooden bench at the edge of the Moss Garden of the Ryoan-Ji in Kyoto and seen how the raked gravel approximates the movement of the waves as they crash motionlessly forever towards the rocks. I might have done better to have seen it on the computer screen, where I would have been less likely, as I sat in mystic contemplation, to have been assaulted by the voices of other Westerners who had also come a long way to look at it yet seemed to have missed the implied requirement for silence and reflection.

If I had been alone with my computer, I could have gone on watching the motionless gravel waves as they moved forever towards the moss-covered rocks. If I sound as if I am repeating myself, it is because I am trying to recapture the appropriate air of concentration, while still not losing the lulling spell of Collins's infectious rhythmic pulse. I recommend the Moss Garden, but only if you can somehow contrive to be alone there. Being the Emperor of Japan would probably be a help in obtaining a solo ticket.

At this point, I should abandon a stretch of prose which is perhaps too influenced by Collins's poetry. (There is a lot to be said, I was going to say at this point, for saying what is not obvious in the tones of the obvious, but much less to be said for saying it too obviously.) (Then I decided not to say that.) Really, in saying that he is homesick even for places where he is, he is saying that there is an ideal that is not extinguished by reality. It's true, alas, and becomes tremendously true on the day that you realise you will have to leave it all. By now in my own life, I have reached the point where Collins's second unnamed poet is the ideal speaker: the one who wrote how much he enjoyed not being able to see his mountain because of the fog. The poet was saying, surely, that he had got to the point where he didn't need the mountain any more because seeing the fog was enough.

The Red Sea

STEPHEN EDGAR

2008

Lulled in a nook of North West Bay,
The water swells against the sand,
Hardly more liquid than Venetian glass,
In which clear surface, just a little way
From shore, some four or five petite yachts pass
With languid ease, apparently unmanned,
Adrift along the day,

Imagining a breeze to fan
Their motion, though there's none. Siobhan
Reaches a giant hand down from the sky
And nudges with insouciant élan
The nearest hull, her bended waist mast-high.
That hand is just as magically withdrawn.
So moves the catamaran.

And through the Lilliputian fleet
She, Beatrice and Gabrielle
Wade in the shallows, knee-deep, spaceman-slow,
To fashion their manoeuvres and compete
Among the stationed hours to and fro,
While watching through the viscid slide and swell
Of water their white feet,

Made curiously whiter by
That cool light-bending element.
Doubled by shadows on the sand they glimpse
Pipefish and darting fingerlings they try
Impossibly to grab, translucent shrimps
Among the lace weed, seahorses intent
To flee the peopled sky.

Hard to conceive that they should be
Precisely who they are and here,
Lost in the idle luxury of play.
And hard to credit that the self-same sea
That joins them in their idleness today,
Careless of latitude and hemisphere,
Blind with ubiquity,

Churns elsewhere with a white uproar,
Or wipes the Slave Coast clean of trees,
Or sucks among the scum and floating drums
Of some forgotten outpost founded for
The advent of an age that never comes,
Or bobs the remnants of atrocities
Limply against the shore.

What luck they have. And what good sense
To leave the water with their toys
When called, before their fortunes are deranged.
And still the day hangs in its late suspense
For hours without them, virtually unchanged,
Until the bay's impregnable turquoise
Relaxes its defence

And sunset's dye begins to spread
In flood across it to the sand
They stood on, as though, hoping to disown
The blood of all the innocents he'd shed,
Macbeth incarnate or his grisly clone
Had stooped on some far shore to rinse his hand,
Making the green one red.

———

I MADE IT TO MY EIGHTIETH BIRTHDAY, BUT IT IS CLEAR
now that I am unlikely to make it much further. So I have decided,
at the time of writing, that this might be the right point to bring
the main part of this book to an end, after eighty poems (more or
less) loved and learned. I might, given time, add a chapter about
how I became a lover of poetry in the first place, back there in an
era when the main buildings of Sydney University were still sep-
arated by grass instead of by more buildings.

But for now it is time to salute Stephen Edgar, who might
soon have to bear alone the burden of being known as Sydney
Technical High School's most prominent poetic alumnus. For
most of my time at the school I had no real idea of what I wanted
to become. (I remember vague dreams of being an aeronautical
engineer: dreams that dissipated of their own accord when it
became clear that I was hopeless at mathematics.) But Edgar
seems to have been preparing himself for a career in poetry from
the very start, and not least when he absorbed whole technical
vocabularies. Few other Australian poets have ever had such a
range of reference to the arts, and fewer still such a precise ana-
lytical knowledge of scientific terminology.

The artistic result of this divine multiple competence might easily have been hard to follow, but in fact he is, from book to book, as clear as the sea water that floats the boats of the little girls in this magnificent poem. You need to know that North West Bay is in southern Tasmania, so the world's oceans ('blind with ubiquity': what a gift of phrase he has) have come a long way in order to provide the background. But otherwise there is only one even remotely obscure reference in it. The reference comes at the end, and turns out to be an invocation of a scene from Shakespeare.

Or perhaps you already knew that 'making the green one red' is Macbeth's follow-up line to 'The multitudinous seas incarnadine'. I myself would have sidelined the ambiguity ('green one' is not just a possible reading, one would have thought, but almost certainly the first reading) by putting in a comma between the 'green' and the 'one red', but I am not Stephen Edgar, nor indeed William Shakespeare. When I look through the splendour of Edgar's work I often wish I were, but you can't have everything; and anyway, that's how all the real poets make you feel, that you wish you could be them. To that extent only, poetry really is a communal enterprise, the conjunction of all our best desires. Whence comes the answer to the perennial question of whether poetry can be evil. The answer is no, not even once. If it ever seems so, then it's another thing.

Postscript:
Growing up in poetical Australia

After citing the poem by Stephen Edgar it is time for me to
bow out, and it might be useful to bring the book full circle
by paying tribute to my homeland, which somehow managed
to inject into us, apparently against all the odds, an awareness
of poetry, a feeling for it. Australia spreads out indefinitely
while only rarely piling up, and even then it seldom piles high:
occasionally there are a few bumps the size of the Cotswolds,
but never even a single Himalaya. From space, which begins
at a low altitude, there is not much down there except rock,
with stretches of scrub for variety. At the edges there is some
green country, but it soon runs into the surf. More often than
not it is hot and bright enough to burn your skin. The whole
layout looks as if it were dreamed up by Dorothea Mackellar
– 'I love a sunburnt country' – except that she makes it too
exciting. The place is huge: as big as America. But you have to
search hard to find anything going on. There is a terrific urge
to get not much done. Yet the Man from Snowy River still
rides.

There was movement at the station, for the word had
    passed around
That the colt from old Regret had got away,
And had joined the wild bush horses – he was worth a
    thousand pound,
So all the cracks had gathered to the fray.

All the tried and noted riders from the stations near
  and far
Had mustered at the homestead overnight,
For the bushmen love hard riding where the wild bush
  horses are,
And the stock-horse sniffs the battle with delight.

That's only the first stanza, and its first line shows that Banjo Paterson had the true measure of the land he lived in. 'There was movement at the station' instead of what you might ordinarily expect: somnolence, and the noise of a few blow-flies attempting to bother a sleeping dog. (Action sequence: the dog gets up and changes position.) It's a tip-off that in Australia, if you are going to write poetry, you must drop your expectations of the day's excitement down to just above the level of a heart's beat.

Yet the poetry of the bush, if not very much of the bush itself, was all around us as we grew up in the cities. Within earshot of the crashing surf, and within sight of the sparkling water, we heard about Paterson's 'The Man from Snowy River'. There was always someone who could recite the whole thing from memory. The poem was so famous that Kirk Douglas was imported briefly in order to star in a movie based on it, thereby adding his stellar gloss to our lacklustre landscape and making this the only book about poetry to mention Kirk Douglas twice.

We also heard about 'The Sick Stockrider' by Adam Lindsay Gordon. 'Clancy of the Overflow', another hard-riding hero, was actually the eponymous Man's sidekick in the Snowy River poem, so it was what the Americans call a twofer. Our teachers, who were usually no more rural than we were, had somehow heard all this stuff about the emptiness out there. Somebody must have enthused about it to them just as they were now enthusing about it to us. Eventually I realised that it was the newspapers that should take the credit. Country newspapers with almost no news to record will often make room for poetry. You will find a boxed-in poem in the middle of the big story about the dog changing position.

One way or another the trick was worked, and by the time I got to university in the late 1950s there were poets all around me. My friend Don Ayrton was the author of two poems. One was:

> Castor and Pollux
> Heavenly twins:
> Neither one knows
> Where the other begins

> Damon and Pythias
> Greatest of friends:
> Neither one knows
> Where the other one ends

> Bound inextricably
> Isn't that funny?
> That's why I only
> Make enemies, sonny.

Like most members of the Downtown Push – a group of lib-ertarian free-thinkers that gathered in the evenings at the Royal George Hotel in Pyrmont so that they could symbolise their defiance of bourgeois society by doing nothing except drink cold beer – Ayrton was a dedicated waster of time. He had long ago forgotten the only other poem he had written. But I learned the one cited above by heart while plying him with schooners of New. (The other kind of beer was called Old.)

Another poet of the Downtown Push was Richard Appleton, otherwise famous for not only writing letters to Ezra Pound, but receiving answers. To do Appleton due credit, it should be recorded that he knew Pound was a maniac. To do Appleton further credit, it should be recorded that his poem 'Barbaree Allen' knocked me so far sideways that I had already half learned it before I got off the floor, and in the next hour I learned the rest, arming myself for life with a party piece fit for the gods.

> Feverish, Barbaree Allen lies
> With wreaths of mist to twist her eyes.
> It won't be long before she dies.
>
> Before she dies, as William did,
> Whose love for her grew old unsaid,
> Examine why she'll soon be dead.
>
> She'll soon be dead, as dead as he,
> And one might argue reasonably
> Blame can't be laid on Barbaree,
>
> Who loved sweet William very well:
> He hastened to his self-made hell
> Because he lacked the wit to tell

Her, take her, bed her down.
He slept with wenches round the town
And found his Wit when she was gone.

When she was gone, Death sidled in:
Friends buried him where she will lie
When dead. They'll rise as roses then.

As roses, then, they'll bloom on trees,
Enjoying, kindly Fate decrees,
Impassioned intercourse, through bees.

I have reproduced the whole thing here because I have an unsettling suspicion that my poor brain might be the only place in which Appleton's masterpiece is still recorded, and it shouldn't be allowed to leave the world with me. You can see this was all life-changing, totally addictive stuff. Further downtown than the Royal George was the Rocks area, once the haunt of C.J. Dennis's hero *The Sentimental Bloke*, forever longing for his girl Doreen. You could chart out the city by the poetry that had happened in it. Somewhere else downtown was another pub, the one where James McAuley had sat playing rag-time piano while working, in his clever head, on the sad rhythms of his great poem 'Because':

My father and my mother never quarrelled.
They were united in a kind of love
As daily as the Sydney Morning Herald,
Rather than like the eagle or the dove . . .

And so on, in a sweep of total brilliance. McAuley, A.D. Hope, Judith Wright and Kenneth Slessor were all actively alive at the time. But the truth remained that the focus of attention was still on what was being done Overseas, and notably in England. Australian poets still ploughed a lonely furrow. It was no wonder that some of them took to drink.

Halfway back up town towards the university, Lex Banning was in Lorenzini's wine bar, as if placed there in position so as to prove how brave a man could be. Lex had cerebral palsy, and in a big way. He could hardly speak at all, yet he wrote exquisite poems. He was the man who taught me, with a single brilliant line of verse, that anglers look like figures from Euclid. I hadn't thought of that myself, and it helped me realise what poetry was for: to get you above yourself. Somewhere in the tangle of two-storey streets must have stood the pub where the poet Harry Hooton had worked on the intricacies of his two-line masterpiece:

> In the midst of life
> We are in Perth

Born and raised in the North Shore suburb of Manly, Bruce Beaver was a poet of Sydney all his life but it was his great poem about the mythical town of 'Hullaboola' that spoke to me most deeply. I can still do that one from memory as well. Here's the whole thing.

> I'm off to Hullaboola
> Where the climate's never cooler
> Than a ringside seat in Hades:
> They grow corn there.
> It pops the while it's growing
> And the reason why I'm going
> Is because I hate the name and wasn't born there.

Yes I'm leaving kin and kith
For that Godforsaken myth
Where Matilda warbles waltzes till she stutters:
Where the dinkum bunyips peer
From their billabongs of beer
And the Clancys overflow into the gutters.

It swung along like a train coming: a characteristic, I like to think, of Australian poetry, which is nearly always a rhythmic event first and foremost. Surprisingly little of it is obscene but it all cracks on. In the Royal George I heard many a scurrilous epic recited but seldom a dirty one. Eskimo Nell never made it that far south: perhaps her kayak got stuck on the Barrier Reef.

Finally the trek back uptown led to the university, where they were waiting for me in a swarm: my poetic contemporaries. Some of them are gone by now – Les Murray went in early 2019. More than sixty years before, I had been literary editor of the student newspaper *honi soit* and busily engaged in accepting and printing my own stuff, when a poem by Murray arrived on my desk.

In my secret garden
I kept three starlings
In my secret locket
Three copper farthings.

One zinc-grey evening
The birds escaped me
And a crippled man stole
My shining money.

The starlings wandered
Till three hawks took them
And now my agents
Have caught the cripple.

Immediately I realised that Murray would do great things. But hey, we all would. We were very young, and our energy was limitless. Few of us are quite that young any more, but those are the breaks. Philip Graham, always known as Chester, whom I haven't seen now for half a century, had so much talent he has never known quite what to do with it. Back in the day when he was pioneering the look of KD trousers, Hong Kong thongs, hog's-bristle crew-cut and a flip-top box of Rothman's filter-tipped cigarettes folded into one short sleeve of his sweatshirt, he wrote a poem that started like this:

From Pilate to Caesar:
If it please your omnipotent godhead
There's an impenient hothead
Questioning you

Look at the way 'impenitent' echoes 'omnipotent': not too exactly but just exactly enough. Or perhaps he wrote 'imperti-nent' instead of 'impenitent': I'm relying on my memory here, and it's starting to fade. Anyway, I was awed by his talent. Unfortunately he wasn't. Given the choice between writing intel-ligibly for the masses and writing unintelligibly for an elite, he chose the latter course, and then spent a lifetime finding out that in Australia there are very few elites, because everyone is equal in a universal disinclination to be patronised. Restless, he went on roaming the world as if it might yield up some context into which he might fit, but now he is home again. When I myself come back it will be in a box of ashes, but I chose the right spot to be born, just as I chose the right profession – poetry – and followed it to the end.

Acknowledgements

I broke the first few square yards of ground on the construction of this book at the same time as I went into hospital for an operation that turned out to be an exercise in chasing a small but speedy cancer around the labyrinthine inner passageways of my increasingly ancient face. If I wanted it to get any more ancient, the medical interventions had to be done, but I woke up to a world in which I could hardly see. Partly as a result I needed a lot of help to get anything written. As in the kind of action movie in which a crack team of ex-soldiers assembles around the grizzled hero – quite often Sylvester Stallone with his mouth on sideways – I pretended to be in command of my advisors, while actually being at their mercy.

My wife Prue Shaw originally had the idea for this book as a combination of critical anthology, teaching aid, hymnal and breviary, and gave a generous amount of time and mental effort to it. My pretending that I was some kind of memory man was always a bit of a joke in the light of what she could do with her own powers of recollection. All the tenacious precision she brings to remembering the verse of Dante she can bring to remembering Wordsworth, and the same powers of analysis along with it. (I have a claim to be better as a go-to man on the moderns, but I would be less than nowhere if I couldn't claim to be better at least at something. Humility must have its limits, or else your modest shuffle backwards culminates with the clamour of broken musical instruments as you plummet from the stage.)

As so often during our lives in each other's orbit, she helped me to remember that poetry is largely a matter of precision. More unusually for a professional scholar, however, she remembers that it is also a matter of imagination, on the part of both writer and reader. And on the wings of her long mission to civilise the man she married, she helped him realise that his final trek to the exit should be a contribution to knowledge, rather than just a celebration of himself. He had long ago done more than enough of that.

Our elder daughter Claerwen inherited a lot of her mother's receptivity and close care for the nuts and bolts of anything that is made. Poetry is a made thing above everything else, so she has proved to be this book's ideal editorial curator. For a large part of the total manuscript she was not only doing the typing, but pointing out the small errors and asking the large questions. There were times when I could generate individual passages of a note, but its higher architecture was sometimes beyond me. She became adept at assembling coherent prose from a heap of bits and pieces. In other words, she has been my chief of staff in the scriptorium. She has also saved my life on quite a few occasions.

It was handy to have on hand my son-in-law Jonathan Grove, whose powers of googling were as helpful as they were daunting. He has also been admirably forbearing with my more or less living in his kitchen for the past five years.

I have been exceptionally lucky in my neighbours this past decade. Deirdre Serjeantson has been crossing the road to visit me and talk about poetry every few mornings for several years. She has a disturbing habit of remembering crucial scholarly details more accurately than I can, but I forgive her. What a great pleasure these conversations have been.

For the past two years, Deborah Meyler walked a few steps down the hill on the same errand even more frequently than that. In the early stages of working on the book, when I could still see hardly a thing, I found to my admiration and alarm that her powers of memory for verse were far superior to my own. Even more annoyingly, she had powers of judgement to match. Together we picked over the poems and fragments of poem that I thought of including – often agreeing and often, thrillingly, disagreeing. Our disputes filled the air far into the evening.

Without any one of these people this book would not have been possible. However I make special mention of Deborah. Our meeting of minds on the subject of poetry has been one of the great satisfactions of my last years. Any errors of fact or objectionable opinions, however, are entirely my own responsibility.

As we worked, all the time I was seeing better, until, first gradually and then suddenly, I could once again see the look of a book, the shape of a column of verse on the page. What magic it still is. It might well add up to the last beautiful thing I see before the lights go out for good. The deadly tunnel merchant in my face won't be giving up even if they bomb him with atomic rays, but there might still be time, and the urgent strength, to catch up with the recently emerged poems or even to write another few poems of my own.

For an unexpected extra decade of life I must thank the staff of Addenbrooke's Hospital, Cambridge. In particular: Dr George Follows, Consultant Haematologist, Dr I. Ringshausen, Honorary Consultant Haemotologist, Gwyn Stafford and Sarah Behan, Specialist Nurses in Haematology, and all the staff of the Haematology and Oncology Outpatients Clinic; Dr Dinakantha Kumararatne, Consultant Immunologist and fellow poetry enthusiast; Professor Edwin Chilvers, Consultant Chest Physician; Dr Mike Allison, Consultant Hepatologist; Dr Richard Benson, Consultant Oncologist; Caroline Hough, Skin Cancer Specialist Nurse; the nursing staff in the Plastic Surgery Unit. I would like to mention particularly Anna, Emma, and all the other nurses of the G2 Infusion Suite. There are many others whose kindness I remember but not their names.

I wish to thank also Jose Fernando Remedios and Richard Gidongo who helped me to continue to live independently at home with my books for the past eighteen months.

The note accompanying 'Canoe' by Keith Douglas: I wrote this note in 2014 at the kind invitation of Anthony Holden as a contribution to his anthology, *Poems That Make Grown Men Cry*. I have expanded it here.

Afterword: Unquenchably Verbal

In the last ten months of his life, extremely frail, unable to see much, paralysed down one side of his face, my father wrote this book. It was characteristic of him that he should use time that seemed already to be filled to capacity – in this case the arduous business of dying – to write something. *The Fire of Joy* is somewhere between a memoir and an anthology: a poignant and very funny celebration of my father's life-long love affair with poetry. At one point in the book he describes his much younger self as 'unquenchably verbal'. That quality persisted until the very end, outlasting more or less every other faculty. What a relief that would have been to him. His facility with words was a gift and a mystery – he didn't know where it came from and sometimes worried that it might one day just as inexplicably desert him. In fact it never did, seeming rather to be some fundamental part of his being, like the beating of his heart or the circulation of his blood, which only failed when they did.

Dad's other unquenchable power was that of appreciation. He was a great *appreciator*, a better word than 'critic', since all worthwhile critics are really in the business of the discernment and celebration of excellence in a field of human endeavour which they love. Poetry was his first and longest love, and *The Fire of Joy* is the expression of that. He hoped it would act as a guidebook for the poetically uninitiated, the nervous, the interested-but-embarrassed. Poetry should not be the preserve of the earnest, the pretentious or the deliberately obscure, he believed.

It is music. The subtitle of the book is 'Roughly 80 Poems to Get by Heart and Say Aloud': he hoped it would get people up on their feet, declaiming.

My father was ill for a long time, and with a bewildering array of maladies. Our sense of fairness or justness dictates that medical misfortunes, like other calamities, should by rights come singly, if at all. But it turns out that that is the perspective of robust youthful health. In practice, when one bit of you goes definitively wrong, it starts a sort of cascade. Other bits of you can't cope with the additional strain, or the effects of the treatment for the first problem, and before you know it, you're getting to know the ropes of a second clinic, elsewhere in the hospital, with totally different rules, procedures, culture, personnel, hours of operation and lingo.

By the end my father was pretty intimately acquainted with the workings of the Oncology, Haematology, Respiratory, Hepatology, Immunology, and Dermatology Departments at our local hospital, with additional significant though finite encounters with Ophthalmology, Plastic Surgery, and Psychiatry. He enjoyed the company of the staff and liked making them laugh, but couldn't have cared less about the details of his ailments or the treatments with which they hoped to fix them. He took me along as a sort of interpreter: a relayer of facts and comprehender of boring technical information.

His first brush was with Renal Medicine, about eleven years ago. It was alarming at the time, but later came to seem routine and unexceptional – a perfectly ordinary problem (enlarged prostate) that they knew how to fix. True, it had nearly killed him, but that was really down to his pathological fear of doctors and lack of insight into the workings of the human body. Most people would have sought help a little earlier when they found themselves unable to pee and it wouldn't have got as far as incipient kidney failure. Dad's keenness to evade any medical procedures that might be looming combined with a reluctance to dramatize or waste someone else's valuable time led to unhelpful downplaying of salient information. In this case, the GP's question 'Have you been having trouble passing urine?' was met with 'Well – a bit.' The canny doctor in A&E a few days later asked a question that required a more objective answer: 'How many teaspoons of urine have you passed in the last seventy-two hours?' to which the answer was 'No teaspoons.'

During that first hospital stay, routine observations uncovered more sinister conditions than the one he was in there to have fixed. His long-term cough turned out to be chronic obstructive pulmonary disease. His blood tests showed that he had chronic lymphocytic leukaemia. Both are incurable. He had abruptly left the land of the well, and entered new territory. And over the course of the next few months, things began to snowball: it seemed he wouldn't be inhabiting this new territory for long. The COPD meant that he couldn't fly. He went to New York by boat instead, but kept to his cabin to avoid the on-board entertainment: the three days of immobility hospitalised him with a huge blood clot in his leg. The leg was never the same again, and he never again left the UK. A few months later an acute chest infection led to another long hospital stay. After his release the steroids that were part of that treatment induced a florid psychosis and he was back in hospital – this time incarcerated in the closed psychiatric ward for ten weeks, his verbal flights having escalated from unquenchable to unhinged. Many hospitalisations for chest infections followed in the years after – recovery taking longer each time, with steroids now removed from the armoury of usable weapons.

All writers, he used to say, have a chip of ice in the heart, because they look upon other people's misfortunes, and their own, and think: 'I could make something out of that.' It's all material: take notes. Now he really had a subject. He lay in a hospital bed in New York and twice a day my four-year-old daughter and I visited him so that she could tickle his feet. That week he wrote the poem 'Whitman and the Moth' about the poet, in old age, meeting oblivious new life. It was the beginning of a great outpouring of poems: about regret, about illness and the approach of death, about the extraordinary beauty of the world and its inexorable renewal, that pierces you so absolutely as you prepare to leave.

His world shrank. As his immune system began to fail due to the leukaemia, he became tethered to the hospital: unable to go away for long because of the need for regular transfusions. Low oxygen saturation steadily reduced the distance he could walk. His excursions were reduced to shuffling, very slowly, the few hundred yards into town to the second-hand bookstall on the market. He adored it. Then that became too much, but he had a terrace which caught the morning sun: he sat there every morning in a state of ecstasy, bathing in the light. 'Send it down, Hughie.' When it rained he loved that too. He never complained: as his horizons became smaller the things still within them became more precious. He interpreted pretty much everything as good luck. He was astonished and thrilled by being still alive to witness the flowering of television into a really serious art-form, thirty years after he stopped being a television critic because he thought he might have said everything there was to say. He wrote a book about that.

Right through his years of illness, a recurrent irritation had been the little skin carcinomas, no longer kept in check by his non-functional immune system, which sprang up regularly on his head and chest, irradiated so thoroughly by the Australian sun sixty years before. They had to be removed lest they escape inwards and become more threatening. In this way he lost the top half of one ear and some fairly large chunks of forehead and shoulder. It was a minor inconvenience compared with everything else that was going on, though there was a relentless quality to the erosion. I told him once about a rather good, but horrifying, low-budget film I had seen about two divers left behind in the open ocean who are slowly nibbled to death by fish. He thought that sounded a bit close to the bone and that he'd give it a miss.

In fact, to the astonishment of all concerned, he lived very nearly a whole decade from that first diagnosis, dying at the respectable age of eighty. 'Apart from being so very, very ill,' said one of his doctors once, 'you have the constitution of the pro-verbial ox.' His favourite haematologist, who substituted friendliness and lack of guile for the usual reserved bedside manner, announced one day what a pleasure it was to see him – jolly well done – every other participant in the experimental leukaemia therapy trial had now died and he was the sole sur-vivor. Slightly taken aback, Dad decided to accept this in the congratulatory spirit with which it was intended. Against all the odds, his heart continued to beat and his gut to function. Perhaps a lifetime of doubtful Cornish pasties and boil-in-the-bag cod in parsley sauce had inured him to problems in that department. Almost every medicine he took – and there were usually six or seven types of pill, several times a day – came festooned with warnings about nausea and upset digestion, but had no such effect on him, not even the chemotherapy or the giant doses of daily antibiotics to fend off the ever-present threat of another respiratory infection. But when infections did occur, as they regularly did, the hospitalisations were no joke. He began to loathe being in hospital. He wanted to be at home, with his books around him, and people that he knew. Two years before he died he signed an end-of-life plan saying that in the event of another infection he did not want to be hospitalised again: he would have only those treatments that could be delivered at home, and if that meant he died, then that was OK.

In February last year a carcinoma which had been removed from his temple the previous September recurred on his cheek. The recurrence was a bad sign, and so was the speed with which this offspring of the original lesion grew. The operation to remove it, and all the lymph nodes to which it might have already migrated in his neck, took eight hours. He woke more or less blind, disfigured, disorientated and very uncomfortable.

Through all the years of his illness, he had been able to read. Now that consolation was no longer possible. He was thrown back on his memory. Poems and fragments of poems long remembered rose to the surface and he brought them out to savour. If a line or phrase was missing he wanted to be reminded what came next. The Italians have a word for this, he said: a *gazofilacio*, the store of poems you remember, the treasure chamber of the mind.

Friends were required to rouse out books from shelves he could no longer reach, find forgotten verses of poems he knew parts of, and then read the whole thing aloud as he sat enraptured. It was like reading to my daughter when she was little: 'Again! Again!' Our friend and neighbour, the novelist Deborah Meyler, was his particular ally – a fellow addict, with a store of remembered poetry that rivalled his own. He would reminisce about when he first heard a poem or what he thought about the author or the poem's construction. He had very little energy so these anecdotes were fragmented. 'I need to nap now, but later I'll tell you a funny story about William Empson and a packet of crisps.' We started writing down what he said so as to be able to go on having the conversation later if he fell asleep in the middle. Deborah was a confident reader, but some of us (yours truly, for example) weren't much in the way of reading poetry aloud and required instructions – these seemed worth writing down too. ('1. Go more slowly than you think you need to. It's because you're ahead of yourself that you stumble.')

The reading aloud was, to me at least, a revelation. There is a small stock of poems I'm fond of. There are even a couple I know by heart. But generally, avid prose reader that I am, I have shied away from poetry as being too rarefied, obscure, obfuscatory, and embarrassing. In ordinary circumstances I would run a mile rather than attend a poetry reading, let alone read it aloud myself. These weren't ordinary circumstances, so I buckled down. The instructions helped: no mention was made of the need for interpretation. He was basically saying: read it the way it's written, and the rhythm will do the interpreting for you. You don't need to add anything to the words. I remember the moment when I really got it. We were reading 'Dover Beach', and the music of it just took over. It's when you get to the 'melancholy, long, withdrawing roar' that it becomes an out of body experience. At the end we were both in tears, and I was hooked.

Over time a manuscript, of sorts, began to assemble itself. As months went by he began to recover from the onslaught of the operation, the terrifying wound slowly healed, and his faculties returned. To be working on a book was his natural state of being – and here to hand was the book on which he was clearly now working: his *gazofilacio*, an anthology of best-loved poems, with autobiographical notes. It so happened that my mother had long been urging him to compile an anthology of this sort – in his words, 'a combination of critical anthology, teaching aid, hymnal and breviary'. Clearly, it was meant to be. Gradually he became able to stay awake for longer and see a little better. Once his keyboard was equipped with giant stick-on letters, he could even type. He moved very slowly between his desk and his dilapidated easy chair, where he sat silently for hours at a time, sometimes asleep, sometimes in a sort of waking dream, apparently seeing with perfect clarity scenes from his childhood and his youth. As the months passed it also became clear that the operation had not been a complete success, that some of the tumour remained, and was growing fast. No further treatment was possible. So this was not just *a* book, but the *last* book.

Into it he poured gratitude and appreciation: appreciation for the poems he loved and which brought him such consolation; gratitude to Australia, the land of his birth, which had introduced him to them. (At the Opportunity school in Sydney in the early 1950s, each child had had to stand beside his desk at the end of the day and recite the poem he or she had been set to learn by heart. Later, at university, poetry was where it was at. He met my mother there: both seemed to have absorbed entire something called the *Albatross Book of Living Verse* which they viewed as a sacred text.) He was grateful, too, for a long life well-lived; for 'this great, good world', and all the things in it, despite his piercing regret to be leaving it. He did not want to die, but he knew this end was no tragedy. 'I've had far, far more than my fair share,' he said.

It began to be very hard to eat: his swallow didn't work very well. We identified the range of foods that could be eaten without difficulty: nothing more challenging than rice pudding. No matter: he really liked rice pudding. The hospital obligingly agreed to pin up the drooping paralysed eyelid of his one good eye. Armed with an astonishing pair of thick spectacles with solid black rims, like Edna in *The Incredibles*, he was suddenly able to read again, not just on the enormously magnified computer screen but smallish type in an actual book. It was a great satisfaction. But every day he was more tired: he read a little, he slept more. *The Fire of Joy* had been sent off to the publisher: he awaited a verdict. Some suggested improvements came back from Don Paterson, his beloved editor at Picador. Did he really want to include that poem by Kingsley Amis – wasn't it a bit misogynist? Had he meant not to include any Robert Burns? He roused himself to respond. Yes, he really *did* want to include the Amis – he rewrote the note to explain why. *Of course* Burns must be in there – the whole of 'Tam o' Shanter' in fact. He sat and typed the note laboriously with a single finger, checking each letter before he hit it. When he got too tired he dictated to me, watching the text unspooling on the screen as he spoke. It was October 23rd. 'That's good,' he said. 'That'll do.' We hit 'send'. 'I'm so tired,' he said. 'I think I'll sit down.' He shuffled over to his easy chair and sat down, and never really left it again.

Claerwen James

2020

Index of first lines

Permission Acknowledgements

The publishers gratefully acknowledge the following for permission to reproduce copyright material.

Kingsley **Amis**, 'A Bookshop Idyll' by Kingsley Amis. Copyright © 1979, Kingsley Amis, used by permission of The Wylie Agency (UK) Limited.   W. H. **Auden**, 'September 1, 1939', from *Another Time*. Copyright © 1940 by W. H. Auden, renewed. Reprinted by permission of Curtis Brown, Ltd.   Bruce **Beaver**, 'I'm off to Hullaboola' (Brandl & Schlesinger, 1999). Reproduced by permission of Brandl & Schlesinger.   John **Berryman**, 'Dream Song 4 – "Filling her compact & delicious body"', from *The Dream Songs* by John Berryman (Faber and Faber Limited).   Norman **Cameron**, 'Green, Green is El Aghir', from *Collected Poems and Selected Translations*, ed. Warren Hope and Jonathan Barker (Carcanet).   Donald **Davie**, 'Remembering the Thirties', from *Collected Poems* (Carcanet).   Carol Ann **Duffy**, 'Mrs Midas', from *The World's Wife* (Picador, 1999), copyright © Carol Ann Duffy 1999.   Stephen **Edgar**, 'The Red Sea', by permission of the author.   T. S. **Eliot**, 'La Figlia Che Piange', from *The Complete Poems and Plays* by T. S. Eliot (Faber and Faber Limited).   William **Empson**, 'Missing Dates', Seventeen (17) lines from *The Complete Poems* by William Empson (Allen Lane 2001) (Penguin Books 2001) Copyright © The Estate of William Empson, 2000. Reproduced with permission of Curtis Brown Group Ltd, London on behalf of the Beneficiaries of the Estate of William

Empson Copyright © William Empson 1937.   U. A. **Fanthorpe**, 'Not My Best Side', by permission of the Estate of U. A. Fanthorpe and Enitharmon Press as publishers of U. A. Fanthorpe's *Selected Poems*.   Robert **Frost**, 'The Silken Tent', from *The Collected Poems* by Robert Frost published by Vintage Classics. Copyright © 1969 by Holt, Rinehart and Winston, Inc. Reprinted by permission of The Random House Group Limited.   Thom **Gunn**, 'On the Move' and 'Listening to Jefferson Airplane', from *Collected Poems* by Thom Gunn (Faber and Faber Limited).   Gwen **Harwood**, 'Last Meeting'. *Gwen Harwood: Selected Poems* by Gwen Harwood Text Copyright © Gwen Harwood First published by Penguin Books Australia 2001 Reprinted by permission of Penguin Random House Australia Pty Ltd.   Seamus **Heaney**, 'Shore Woman', from *Opened Ground* by Seamus Heaney (Faber and Faber Limited).   Anthony **Hecht**, "Japan", from *Collected Earlier Poems* by Anthony Hecht, copyright © 1990 by Anthony E. Hecht. Used by permission of Alfred A. Knopf, an imprint of the Knopf Doubleday Publishing Group, a division of Penguin Random House LLC. All rights reserved.   David **Holbrook**, 'Poor Old Horse', from *Selected Poems* (Carcanet).   Brian **Howard**, 'Gone to Report', from *The Golden Horizon*, ed. Cyril Connolly (Weidenfeld & Nicolson): all our attempts at tracing the copyright holder of 'Gone to Report' by Brian Howard were unsuccessful.   Ted **Hughes**, 'Pike', from *Lupercal* by Ted Hughes (Faber and Faber Limited).   Randall **Jarrell**, 'The Death of the Ball Turret Gunner', from *The Complete Poems* by Randall Jarrell Copyright © 1969, renewed 1997 by Mary von S. Jarrell. Reprinted by permission of Farrar, Straus and Giroux. All rights Reserved.   Galway **Kinnell**, Excerpt from 'The Avenue Bearing the Initial of Christ into the New World', from *The Avenue Bearing the Initial of Christ into the New World* by Galway

Kinnell. Copyright © 1954, 1960, renewed 1982, 1988 by Galway Kinnell. Reprinted by permission of Houghton Mifflin Harcourt Publishing Company. All rights reserved.   Philip **Larkin**, 'An Arundel Tomb', from *The Complete Poems* by Philip Larkin (Faber and Faber Limited). 'Will Not Come Back' from *Collected Poems* by Robert **Lowell**. Copyright © 2003 by Harriet Lowell and Sheridan Lowell. Reprinted by permission of Farrar, Straus and Giroux. All Rights Reserved.   James **McAuley**, 'Because', By Arrangement with the Licensor, The James McAuley Estate, c/- Curtis Brown (Aust) Pty Ltd.   Louis **MacNeice**, 'Snow' and 'The Sunlight on the Garden' © Estate of Louis MacNeice, reprinted by permission of David Higham.   John **Masefield**, 'Cargoes', by permission of The Society of Authors as the Literary Representative of the Estate of John Masefield.   Marianne **Moore**, 'The Paper Nautilus', from *The New Collected Poems of Marianne Moore* (Faber and Faber Limited).   Dom **Moraes**, 'At Seven O'Clock', from *In Cinnamon Shade* (Carcanet).   Les **Murray**, 'In My Secret Garden', from *New Collected Poems* (Carcanet).   Dorothy **Parker**, 'One Perfect Rose', copyright 1926, renewed © 1954 by Dorothy Parker; from *The Portable Dorothy Parker* by Dorothy Parker, edited by Marion Meade. Used by permission of Viking Books, an imprint of Penguin Publishing Group, a division of Penguin Random House LLC. All rights reserved.   Sylvia **Plath**, 'The Cut' from *Collected Poems* by Sylvia Plath (Faber and Faber Limited).   Ezra **Pound**, 'And the days are not full enough' and 'In a Station of the Metro', by Ezra Pound, from *Personae*, copyright © 1926 by Ezra Pound. Reprinted by permission of New Directions Publishing Corp., and Faber and Faber Limited.   Frederic **Prokosch**, 'War of Nerves', copyright © Frederic Prokosch 1940.   Henry **Reed**, 'The Naming of Parts', from *Collected Poems* (Carcanet).

Vita **Sackville-West**, 'The Craftsmen' (from *The Land*) © Vita Sackville-West, 1926. Reproduced by permission of Curtis Brown Group Ltd. on behalf of the Estate of Vita Sackville-West. Wallace **Stevens**, 'The Emperor of Ice-Cream', from *Collected Poems* by Wallace Stevens (Faber and Faber Limited). Dylan **Thomas**, 'In my craft or sullen art', from *The Collected Poems of Dylan Thomas: The Centenary Edition* (Weidenfeld & Nicolson), copyright © The Dylan Thomas Trust. 'Sea Grapes' from *Sea Grapes* by Derek **Walcott**. Copyright © 1976 by Derek Walcott. Reprinted by permission of Farrar, Straus and Giroux. All Rights Reserved.